D0290328

BEYOND THE HILL

A Directory of Congress
from 1984 to 1993
Where Have All the Members Gone?

By Rebecca Borders and C.C. Dockery

University Press of America, Inc.
Lanham • New York • London

University Press of America®, Inc.
4720 Boston Way
Lanham, Maryland 20706

3 Henrietta Street
London WC2E 8LU England

Copublished by arrangement with
The Center for Public Integrity

Library of Congress Cataloging-in-Publication Data

ISBN 0-8191-9819-6 (cloth)
ISBN 0-8191-9820-X (paper)

♾™ The paper used in this publication meets the minimum
requirements of American National Standard for Information
Sciences—Permanence of Paper for Printed Library Materials,
ANSI Z39.48–1984.

A000000b404215

Dedication

Beyond the Hill is appreciatively dedicated to the members of Congress whose names appear on these pages. Many are men and women of great achievement. Several have given years of their lives, talents and time, serving with great distinction. Some have wandered off the path of devoted public service after having travelled a laudable distance down the road of duty and honor to country. All, however, have participated in our wonderful and unique political system. Without them, Democrats, Republicans and Independents, the system would not survive. To each and every one of those chronicled here, to their families and friends, we say "thanks" for having given life to the words, "Democracy In Action." We wish you the very best.

Contents

Foreword

I believe it when the polls and general observation tell me that Americans are "mad as hell" these days. We lash out at politicians, it seems, because they are an easy target on whom to take out our frustrations. And, well, they also deserve it. The betrayal committed by many cynical politicians is to promise that they really care about the issues and the people in their home districts, while their attention is focused somewhere inside the Beltway. Too often, long-time members of Congress have houses in the Washington area that are larger and more lived-in than the one-room apartment "back home." This set of circumstances has become, if not widely applicable, the cliché.

The cliché is extended when we turn it into the "conventional wisdom" that upon leaving Congress, for whatever reason, members stay in Washington. What further proof of the cynicism and betrayal is needed? As it turns out, a lot more is needed to make the case that when members of Congress serve for a long time they forget their roots or the reasons they sought to represent their constituents. We rarely, probably because we don't go to the trouble, glimpse into the minds of our elected representatives to see what they think about their service and its philosophical underpinnings. Our assumption has usually been that people seek to get elected to the House or Senate because they want power. That is almost universally true, but there's a great deal more to the whole dynamic of why someone like Roy Dyson, for example, would still want to represent his district, this time in the Maryland state house, after having to leave the U.S. Congress because of speculation and scandal reported in the media.

This book tries to communicate that great deal more. What *Beyond the Hill* shows is that everyone who sought to become a member of Congress shared one motivation: Power. Part of what we hope to show here is that many members gave great consideration to what it means to seek power, then to exercise it (or attempt to) and finally to lose it or give it up. The full range of human emotion is on display in *Beyond the Hill*. From the arrogance of a one-termer to the awe of an old-timer to the gentility of one who inherited the office, we hope you get the idea that Congress is not monolithic and that differing ideas still have a place. That said, some of the ideas clearly show some members and former members of Congress to be the venal sellouts that many voters think they are.

What we found out when Rebecca Borders and C.C. Dockery took a look at what happened to 353 members of Congress who served between 1984 and 1993 is that many left Washington to go back to where they ran from and resumed practicing law or farming or selling lumber. We also found that of the 99 former lawmakers who stayed in Washington, 82 percent (81) of them became lobbyists. Go figure.

So why is it that the "conventional wisdom" has most former members taking up new offices along K Street's lobbying corridors? The reason could be that most of the political writers in the country tend to hang out in Washington and talk to others who stay here. The mistake might be in looking at this conventionally in the first place. That's probably another book. *This* book, *Beyond the Hill*, we hope, is not conventional. We think that those members of Congress who didn't get reelected can learn what life is about to be like. We hope the book evokes some thoughtful consideration of how the people who make up Congress work and think. If not, then just use the directory to send a letter saying you're mad as hell.

Alejandro Benes
Managing Director
The Center for Public Integrity
Washington, D.C.

Preface

There is a story that floats around Washington about an ambitious political science professor. Years ago, this professor, had approached a number of think tanks with a proposal for a study of where members of Congress go after they leave office. In his proposal, the professor included a budget for travel. The response from each of the think tanks was the same: why do you need a travel budget when all of the former lawmakers are in the same two-block area of K Street in downtown Washington?

The K Street corridor is notorious as a haven for some lawmakers-turned-lobbyists, but not a majority. So, where do the most Representatives and Senators go after they leave Congress?

This book chronicles where many Capitol Hill lawmakers are living, what they are doing, and the circumstances under which they left Congress.

Our study group consists of 353 Representatives and Senators who began or finished their congressional service between 1984 and 1993. The research, which was conducted from January 1993 through November 1994, consisted of telephone interviews, personal visits, questionnaires, searches of electronic news libraries, and reviews of lobbying reports filed with the House and Senate, and foreign agent registration papers on record with the Department of Justice.

The House bank scandal, Iran-Contra hearings, the resignations of the House Speaker James Wright and Majority Whip Tony Coehlo for financial irregularities, and the Clarence Thomas confirmation hearings all occurred between 1984 and 1993. And with each controversy, the nation's distrust of Congress grew.

In a 1992 nationwide poll by ABC News, 82 percent of the respondents surveyed agreed with the statement, "Generally speaking, those we elect to Congress in Washington lose touch with the people pretty quickly."

In our focus group of 353 lawmakers, 15 currently serve in Congress, one is vice president. A surprisingly low 26 percent (93) became active lobbyists. But of the *former* lawmakers who stayed in Washington (99), 82 percent (81) worked as lobbyists. Nine were registered foreign agents.

Of those who left the capital, the career choices are as diverse as the ex-lawmakers themselves: former Rep. James McClure Clarke (D., N.C.) raises raspberries and apples on his farm in North Carolina; former Rep. Roy Dyson (D., Md.) works in his family's hardware store and has just launched a return to politics, former Rep. Delbert Latta (R., Ohio) spends time with his grandchildren and takes Automobile Association of America-sponsored trips with his wife; former Sen. Alan Dixon (D., Ill.) is a partner is a St. Louis-based law firm; and former Rep. Ron Paul (R., Texas) is delivering babies as a practicing obstetrician in Lake Jackson, Texas.

Fourteen members moved from the House to the Senate; ten moved from Congress to governorships; two went from the House to mayor's offices; seven were appointed to Cabinet positions; three were appointed ambassadors, and two became Vice Presidents. Six have been convicted of felonies and have ended up in prison. Thirty died either in office or after their service was over.

From 1984 to 1993, 136 members of the House and Senate lost their bids for reelection or failed in attempts to gain other offices. Of these, 41 percent (55) stayed in the Washington area.

Representative Neil Abercrombie (D., Hawaii) lost his 1986 reelection bid, but came back to win again in 1990 and currently serves in the House.

At this writing, former Representatives Dick Cheney and Jack Kemp along with former Senator and Vice President Dan Quayle, are contemplating presidential bids for 1996.

Based on this study of the 353, it seems the political science professor may have needed a bit of a travel allowance after all.

Acknowledgements

This book would not have been possible without the support and encouragement of many people. Keith Lee Rupp and Pauline Borders provided valuable inspiration and enormous patience. Paula Dockery helped with the selection of the title. And many thanks to Vicky Farris for helping with the organization and presentation of the material.

The brilliant staff at the Center for Public Integrity performed miracles daily: Margaret Ebrahim, Diane Renzulli, Robert Schlesinger, Amy Bohm, Alex Knott, Thomas Greving and Marianne Szegedy-Maszak. A special thank you goes to Charles Lewis and Alejandro Benes for their encouragement throughout the process.

Our gratitude extends to the staff at the National Journalism Center, especially Mal Kline, for generously sharing their time and equipment; to Bill Hogan and Gwen McLin for their kind and almost painless editing; to all those who provided backup on the project: Peter Roff, Scott Wahlin, Pam Woods Sarich, Janice Sperry, Ann Baldinger and Elizabeth Lewis; and to William and Betsy Rupp for their understanding.

Introduction

Are members of Congress really addicted to politics? Seduced by power? Consumed by the need to raise huge amounts of campaign money? If congressional service can mean putting everything on the line -- family, financial security, and personal reputation -- why do members fight so hard to stay in office? According to a former representative, congressional service can turn into a vicious cycle of fund-raising and campaigning for reelection that leaves little time for anything else.

Most of the former members of Congress interviewed for this book said that they feel enormous relief when their political careers are over. This isn't to say that most lawmakers don't experience depression after defeats or don't miss the power, perks, and prestige that can go along with congressional service. But no matter how long their terms, most conceded that the daily grind of congressional life had worn them out.

What about life away from the Capitol? What do lawmakers do after they have, in many cases, devoted their adult lives to politics? Do they go back home and try to resume their past lifestyles? Do they use their government experience to build more lucrative careers as lobbyists?

And what happens emotionally to members of Congress who are suddenly thrown out of office? To lose your job is painful, but to lose it in such a public manner can be humiliating. Many politicians go through year-long depressions after losing their reelection bids. Even those who retire have found that readjusting to average life can be painful. "It is a real shock," said former Representative Jim Coyne (R., Pa.) who is a director of the Former Members of Congress Association. "A lot go through tremendous depression and cling to the trappings. They've got to have the fancy offices, staff, people to shuttle them to the airports. This is a real shock."

No more crowds, no more campaign signs or bumper stickers, and usually no more headlines. Often the public memory consists only of the vague recognition of constituents.

Is there happiness "Beyond The Hill?" Most ex-members, said that they are happier out of congressional life and would not run for public office again."I'm trying to pay all of the bills I accumulated in Congress," former Representative Webb Franklin (R., Miss.) joked. "My wife would shoot me if I ran again."

Former Representative Jack Buechner (R., Mo.), who stayed in Washington to work as a lobbyist after his 1990 defeat, wrote to us that: "At night, when Congress is in session, if I see the light in the dome, I ache for the halcyon times, no matter how few. But when I walk into my home, see my wife, Nancy, and our infant son, Charlie, I question if it is worth the price to serve in today's Congress. I am proud to have served, but happy that I am no longer there."

For some former members, life after Congress can be financially rewarding because of their "golden parachutes," including leftover campaign funds that before the 103rd Congress could be converted to personal use. Government pensions can run into the millions of dollars for longtime members over the course of their retirement.

The relief from political pressure may be some consolation for the loss of congressional perquisites. Lawmakers on Capitol Hill are "members," as though they are part of an elite club. And they are. Signs above elevators and at certain entrances to the Capitol proclaim "Members Only" or "Only Members and Staff Beyond This Point." Policemen stationed along Independence and Constitution Avenues halt traffic so that members can hurry to the Capitol to vote. Members have free parking in their office buildings, at Washington's two airports, and often the airports in their home districts, too. If they light up a cigarette or cigar in a no-smoking federal building, no one raises an eyebrow.

Yet the life of a Senator or Representative is by no means easy. The never-ending cycle of fund-raising and campaigning takes its toll on even the most energetic members.

"The great dream is to have the job and the power without going through the headache of getting elected," said former Representative Jim Coyne. Coyne is now a term-limits activist and the co-author of the 1992 book *Cleaning House*. "Others are worn out realistically by the dirtiness of the business. Everybody's campaign opponent has someone whose job it is to make your life miserable. No other job, short of being married to Roseanne Arnold, exposes you to that kind of ridicule."

In Washington, the congressional reform movement has been all but stagnant. Senator David Boren (D., Okla.) long a voice against the revolving door, decided to leave Congress in late 1994 to become the president of the University of Oklahoma. His reform legislation, which would have barred former members and congressional aides from lobbying for five years, won little support in the 103rd Congress.

This book includes profiles of former lawmakers who represent a variety of political thought, lifestyles, incomes, and length of service. They are all outspoken, aggressive personalities who have left their own mark on today's political world. They were selected to illustrate several of the more definable experiences of ex-lawmakers: comfortably retired away from Washington politics; vying for higher office; struggling to revive a political career; Washington lobbyists; and retired, but still inside the Capital Beltway.

The listings in the directory summarize the careers of the 350 members of the House and Senate who served from 1984 to 1993.

The summaries are based on interviews, materials submitted to the authors by the members, at the authors' request, and public records. The length of the summaries vary in proportion to the material available. Phone numbers and addresses were taken from public sources.

Former members of Congress may lead varied lives, but they share a common denominator: They have all done more than tasted political power; they dined on it in the grandest halls of America's monuments to democracy. That is their common link.

For former Representative Roy Dyson (D., Md.), the sting of losing his House seat in 1990 was compounded by the scandals that were played out on the front pages of *The Washington Post*. Even though he now lives just 75 miles from Washington, Dyson has never returned to the Capitol and still harbors ill feelings toward the Washington Establishment.

Former Representative Peter Smith (R., Vt.) remained in Washington after his defeat in 1990. But the one-term lawmaker has left politics and returned to his old career as an educator, as the dean of education at the George Washington University. In contrast, Bob Kastenmeier (D., Wis.) served for 16 terms in the House before being caught by surprise by one of the nation's first term limits candidates.

Dick Cheney (R., Wyo.) balked at political convention when he left Washington to run for the House in 1978 from his home state of Wyoming. Today, he is back in Wyoming, where he's plotting a run at the presidency in 1996.

Michael D. Barnes (D., Md.) turned his congressional experience into a big business by representing Jean-Bertrand Aristide, Haiti's President. Bill Gradison (R., Ohio) resigned just weeks after winning reelection to the House in 1992 to become the president of the Health Insurance Association of America. Beryl Anthony (D., Ark.) and Tom Downey (D., N.Y.) were both upset in the 1992 elections in the wake of the House bank scandal. Today, Anthony and Downey, both successful Washington lobbyists, represent clients before their former committees. Former Senator James McClure (R., Idaho) now represents some of the world's most powerful mining concerns.

Lindy Boggs (D., La.) first arrived in Washington as the 24-year-old bride of Representative Hale Boggs. After his plane disappeared in Alaska in 1974, she made the transition from congressional spouse to lawmaker. Lindy Boggs served in the House for 16 years, making her own mark on the predominantly male institution.

The lives of these former lawmakers provide a window into the institution of Congress and people who are drawn to it.

"Enlighten the people generally," Thomas Jefferson wrote in a letter to du Pont De Nemours on April 24, 1816, "and tyranny and oppressions of body and mind will vanish like evil spirits at the dawn of the day."

Hard Feelings: Roy Dyson

Roy Dyson sits in middle age, alone, at the dining room window of the rural Maryland home he shares with his mother and sister. He watches a black limousine cruise over the hill. Inside the limousine is one of Washington's most powerful men: Ben Bradlee, the former executive editor of *The Washington Post*. Bradlee is on his way to his country estate, where the fruits of retirement can be savored after a long, illustrious career.

Inside the dining room, Roy Dyson contemplates his own retirement -- forced, early, and filled with disgrace -- while savoring the irony that has placed one of the architects of this retirement within such proximity. Dyson now plots a return to power. The image was offered by Dyson himself during a series of rare interviews.

Unlike most other former Capitol Hill lawmakers, who never lose their patina of power and respectablility, Dyson has had to start again from scratch. His only hope for regaining a measure of the power he once had is through political redemption. Had he not been tinged by scandal, Dyson might have gotten a job in Washington as a lobbyist or as the president of a major trade association. But it was not to be. Once Dyson became "damaged goods," in the cruel parlance of politics, Washington had little more, if any, use for him.

Dyson was once a powerful man in his own right as a member of Congress. In 1988, however, Bradlee's newspaper published the front page expose on Dyson and his congressional office practices that resulted in a staff member's suicide and Dyson's own brutal, public disgrace.

These days, Bradlee's handyman frequently comes into Dyson's hardware store for supplies. To Dyson, it all seems absurd.

"I have never been back to the Capitol -- no reason to," Dyson said while drinking a cup of coffee in his dining room just 75 miles away from Washington in the tiny southern Maryland community of Great Mills. Dyson, who had never moved to Washington, joked that he just made one last commute home. He is quick to point out that except for the Bradlee sightings, he could just as well be a million miles away from Capitol Hill and the political scheming that landed him in trouble and political and personal exile.

Once the wunderkind of Maryland Democratic politics, Dyson was elected to the state House at age 25, and Congress at 31. Today, relaxed at age 45, Dyson says that he has rebounded personally from his 1990 loss. In 1994, he won election to the Maryland Senate.

The Dyson home is a large white colonial occupied by Dyson, his sister, Lynn, and their mother, Marie. It sits atop a hill, overlooking the family hardware store and most of the town of Great Mills. Visitors are greeted by a huge but harmless dog that actually belongs to another sister who lives in a renovated barn toward the back of the property.

The friendly two-story home belonged to Dyson's grandparents. When he was a child, he and his family moved up the hill and into the home. Years later, his sister built a parallel house adjoining the original house so that their mother would not be alone. There are two big kitchens, two dining rooms, and so on. His seven brothers and sisters live within six miles of the home. "The majority are within sight of this house," Dyson said, sweeping his hand toward the rolling hills. Ironically, his twin brother, Lee, works in Washington as a Capitol policeman. They were both named after their father, Leroy.

An antique truck, with "Dyson Hardware" painted on the side, sits under a shed by the driveway. The deck and swimming pool area in the back make one imagine a long summer day, surrounded by dogs, laughing children, and teasing brothers and sisters.

Dyson's life is full of family these days: a nephew applying for college, a brother who needs to use the car, the store to run. Most family members, like Dyson, work in one of the two Dyson Trust Worthy Building Centers. "We're trying just to survive," Dyson said. "We're up against Wal-Mart and Hechinger's [a large hardware chain]. We're trying to stay ahead." The Dyson Building Center is the kind of place where you can have a cup of coffee, catch up with some old friends, and discuss the issues of the day. The employees wear brightly colored T-shirts and greet customers as they walk in the door. The two stores were run by Dyson's father until his death, and now Marie is the chairman of the company.

"Government does absolutely nothing for small business; Congress does nothing," Dyson said. "They deserve an Academy Award for lip service."

Aside from the hardware business, Dyson is still involved in local affairs. Across the road from Dyson's home is the Little Flower Catholic Elementary School, which he and his siblings attended. He has recently helped to organize a school council.

The Dyson family has been in St. Mary's County since the 1600s, and Dyson now serves as the chairman of the board of the St. Clement's Island Museum. "I never would have been able to do it while in office," he said. "I would have never had time." When he presided over the opening of the museum's annual children's day, he appeared somehow refreshed, with lots of smiles on his still boyishly handsome face.

Driving through the area's farmlands, which are dotted with tiny towns and country Catholic churches, Dyson expounded on the rich history of the place that is graced with such natural beauty. During the Civil War, county officials were placed under house arrest by President Lincoln because they were suspected of Southern leanings. A prisoner-of-war camp for captured Confederate soldiers was built at Point Lookout, where the Potomac River flows into the Chesapeake.

During a lunch of crabcakes at the Seaside Restaurant, which is housed in a vacation trailer-park community along the St. Mary's River, Dyson showed that he is still in fine political form. He paused to speak to most of the patrons and chatted with the owner about his views on the Whitewater affair. The customers seemed genuinely happy to see Dyson and to have a chance to talk politics with him, and in return Dyson was as friendly as he could be.

In this down-home setting, it is hard to picture him glad-handing defense lobbyists at fund-raisers. These days, however, lobbyists don't hold much credibility with him. "If I had gone and become a lobbyist, which is to me a dirty word, I would still be jaded," Dyson said.

Maybe it is the same theology that a reformed smoker might have about smoking. Now, during guest lectures to political science students at Charles County Community College, Dyson says that he pounds his fist on the lectern and brandishes this message: "I think *people* ought to become lobbyists. They ought not to be intimidated by a member of Congress or even the President. You run the country. You pay the bills. It is absurd that there are so many people up there making so much money. You can do it yourself. Lobbying distorts the system."

Dyson is open about how he lost touch with the reality of daily living during his years in Congress. "The system is so scarred," he said. "Even though I came home every night, I didn't see that sense of disappointment within the American people. You have no idea how many people are out there hurting and I never saw it while I was in office."

"You really isolate yourself from ordinary people and ordinary Americans. I mean, I don't know what it would be like to have to live in a car. What happens to those people? There are two different Americas, even here in St. Mary's County. I see why people are so cynical. Now I'm becoming cynical."

"Coming home was an incredible learning experience. That was Jefferson's idea, a citizen legislature, a place where people serve for a while."

But Dyson doesn't think much of term limits. "The system is more broken than that," he said. "It doesn't relate. My term was limited. Term limits seem so cosmetic. Look at all the new members who went in 1992. And what changed? They should have turned that place around. What ever really changed? It seems as lobbyists and special interests have an inordinate amount of influence because of fundraising."

A Dyson race for a Maryland State Senate seat could mean a resumption of the career that showed so much promise early on; it would also resurrect memories of dark allegations and the death of a close aide.

To look at Dyson today, one must examine just how his world came crashing down around him. Why he is working in a hardware store instead of holding court as one of Washington's movers-and-shakers.

The beginning of the end of Dyson's congressional career came with the news that his administrative assistant, Tom Pappas, had committed suicide when he leaped to his death from a New York City hotel room the day *The Washington Post* ran a front-page story detailing Pappas's questionable hiring and managerial practices. The scandal and the wild press coverage that followed almost cost Dyson the 1988 election and continue to follow him to this day.

The story centered on Pappas's alleged demands that male staff members attend social events with him and other staff members (Pappas had told one newly hired aide that the job requirements included no dating for one year after joining the staff.) and alleged campaign-finance irregularities, including illegal payments from the Dyson campaign to Pappas and his political consulting business, Pappenbauer Associates.

The most bizarre revelation was that Pappas had taken out an advertisement in the Hannibal, Missouri, *Courier-Post* featuring the headline, "Wanted: A Young Man in a Hurry." The ad went on to read "Are you a young man with big ideas about the rest of your life? Are you single and willing to travel?" A writing sample and a recent photograph were requested from potential candidates, who were to reply to Pappenbauer Associates. The ad was paid for by the Dyson campaign.

Dyson, who was in New York City with Pappas and another aide when the *Post* story broke, was said to be emotionally devastated by the suicide. According to the police report, Dyson said that he was attending a service at St. Patrick's Cathedral at the time of Pappas's death. He defended Pappas during a news conference three days after his death by saying, "Tom was a human being, and we all make mistakes." He also denied knowing about Pappas's recruiting and management techniques.

As rumors flew through the Capitol, Dyson was forced to deny that either he or Pappas were gay (since the story had been full of suggested homosexual activity by the staff). In a single paragraph, the *Post* story had noted that Dyson was unmarried and Pappas was divorced and that Dyson sometimes stayed overnight at Pappas's suburban Maryland home instead of making the hour-and-a-half commute drive to Great Mills.

Katie Tucker, Dyson's press secretary, said at the time that "all of the former aides quoted in the *Post* story had been fired [before the suicide] and had a bone to pick."

Media critics and Dyson supporters questioned the *Post* about the necessity of running such a story on the front page of a Sunday edition when the charges did not directly involve Dyson -- only the apparent problems of Pappas. Dyson is still bewildered about that issue. Although he would not speak of the Pappas ordeal on the record, he questioned why his office was targeted for such intense scrutiny when other administrative assistants and even lawmakers often required staff members to keep social hours with them.

In the *Post's* own "Ombudsman" column one week after the original article and Pappas's subsequent suicide, Richard Harwood wrote: "The story was legitimate. The outcome was a great tragedy for the friends and family of Tom Pappas."

Dyson's wild ride was far from over. In June 1988, he was named in the FBI's "Ill Wind" investigation of defense contractors. A major target of the wide-ranging investigation was Unisys Corporation, a huge Detroit-based electronics and defense manufacturing firm. Dyson and then-Representative Bill Chappell, a Democrat from Florida who chaired the House Appropriations Defense Subcommittee, had sought to continue funding the MK92 Coherent Receiver/Transmitter (CORT) radar system, manufactured by Unisys, even though the Navy had urged Congress to cancel it. Unisys and the Navy are both employers in Dyson's district, and Dyson was a member of the House Armed Services Subcommittee on Seapower. Chappell lost his 1988 reelection bid as a result of the scandal and died less than a year later.

As it turned out, Dyson and Pappas and another staff aide were in New York City on a Unisys-sponsored trip when Pappas died. Dyson had toured the corporation's plant in Great Neck, N.Y., and had had dinner and attended the Broadway show "Phantom of the Opera" with Pappas, the other aide, and Charles F. Gardner, a one-time vice president of Unisys. Dyson agreed to pay for part of the weekend expenses after a speech for which he was to have received an honorarium was canceled because of Pappas' death.

Dyson had accepted thousands of dollars in campaign contributions from Unisys and other defense contractors. No charges were ever brought against Dyson or Chappell, but the allegations had long-term effects.

The FBI released an affidavit from federal wiretaps in October 1990 that linked Gardner to Dyson. Gardner told William Roberts, a former Unisys executive, that there was $95,000 to "take care of any Dysons or anything like that." Gardner was also quoted as saying about the fateful 1988 trip to New York City that "They don't even want to see the plant -- they really want a weekend in New York." On a trip to New York in 1987, Dyson had accepted $17,000 in what he thought were individual contributions. After Gardner was sentenced for his role in the contracting scheme in 1989, Dyson denied knowing that the donations had actually been underwritten by Unisys but acknowledged that accepting them had been a mistake. He returned a total of $19,000 to defense contractors. Thirty-nine corporations and individuals were convicted as a result of the investigation. Gardner received a 32-month prison sentence.

The 1988 campaign featured a hard-hitting effort by the National Republican Congressional Committee to remind voters of Pappas's suicide and the "Ill Wind" scandal. A television ad blanketed the district that featured President Reagan endorsing Dyson's Republican challenger, Wayne Gilchrest. Dyson won the 1988 race by 1,500 votes, but challengers, all smelling blood, came out the political woodwork to take him on in 1990, including a reenergized Gilchrest.

Another round of charges regarding Dyson's personal dealings and his conscientious objector status during the Vietnam War surfaced just before the Democratic primary. Dyson's record stood in direct contradiction to his hawkish stances as a member of the Armed Services committee. Dyson defended his actions, citing his participation in the antiwar movement. "I was a part of that movement . .

and I felt very strongly about it and would still feel that way today," Dyson said in an interview with *The Washington Post.* "I was part of the turmoil of that period."

Despite the revelations, Dyson defeated a strong Democratic rival. The Republican nominee, however, was a different matter, however. Gilchrest, in contrast to Dyson, was a Marine combat veteran who had been awarded a Bronze Star and a Purple Heart for service in Vietnam. One Gilchrest ad asked, "Who do you believe? Roy Dyson? Or veteran, teacher, family man Wayne Gilchrest?"

The ad war heated up. In a Dyson television commercial, Marie Dyson defended her son. "It [the attack on Dyson] hurts all of his family very deeply," she said.

Dyson couldn't recover fast enough to beat Gilchrest again. He lost the election 57% to 43% after spending $771,809, two-thirds of it from PACs. Gilchrest spent just $264,932.

The loss left him $20,000 in debt, disillusioned, and despondent. Dyson spent two months after he left office working the telephones, trying to raise money to pay off his debt. But it isn't easy to raise money for a lost campaign.

Bizarrely enough, it seems that Maryland's 1st Congressional District was somehow destined for scandal. Dyson defeated Republican Bob Bauman in 1980 after Bauman was arrested for soliciting sex from a 16-year-old male prostitute. Bauman, in turn, had replaced Republican William O. Mills after Mills committed suicide in May 1973 following revelations about an unreported $25,000 campaign contribution from President Richard Nixon's Committee to Reelect the President.

As a conservative Democrat, Dyson supported President Reagan's congressional agenda about 50 percent of the time, which fit the politics of his district about perfectly. With a large number of government employees, Dyson's district covered the tobacco-farming hills of southern Maryland up to the fishing villages of the Chesapeake Bay and Eastern Shore to north of Baltimore.

"The thing that most pleases me about my work in Congress was that I introduced the first bill to clean up the Chesapeake Bay," Dyson said. "And I worked on keeping the Patuxent military installation to ensure that jobs were available.

"People still come up to me and say: 'Your office was so open. It was a place to go if you needed help.' I get the most personal satisfaction out of that. People need a place to go for help. Nothing in the world is more heartwarming than if you can help a person who is in an apparently hopeless situation. Looking into the face of someone who was in desperate need and who got help, there is no fund-raiser, no letter from the Speaker, no pat on the back from the President that will match that. I love my district. I love the people, and they felt very comfortable with me."

Not only does Dyson, with his distrust of government, now sound more like a conservative Republican, but he's been invited to speak at county Republican gatherings -- even though he ran as a Democratic in the state Senate race.

He spends his Sunday mornings doing a call-in radio show on WSMP-AM in Mechanicsville, Maryland. On the public affairs show, Dyson and his high-school French teacher discuss politics over coffee and muffins. "We have a lot of fun with it," Dyson said.

Ethics appeared to be a centerpiece of Dyson's campaign for the state Senate. He refused to accept PAC contributions and placed a $100 limit on other donations. When you don't have any money," Dyson said, "you've got to go door to door." His 1994 campaign signs were recycled from the congressional days, just flipped over and repainted. His palm cards still featured "Mother Dyson's recipe for Maryland stuffed ham." And the cover pictured the new Dyson, sitting on a dock, barefoot, pants legs rolled up, holding his nieces and nephews. "In Annapolis," it proclaimed, "they're going to hear two words in 1995: Roy Dyson."

Dyson, the congressional ethics poster child of the late 1980s, says that he has found his way back. Back to his center, his family and his home. And maybe back to what got him into politics in the first place: doing the right thing.

But the hard feelings of those years of rumors and innuendo, mistakes, and political miscalculations will not fade for years to come.

"There is a great wealth of people out there," Dyson, the small businessman, said. "America is a great country if government doesn't get in the way."

Starting Over: Peter Smith

"The initial reality is that you're unemployed," Peter Smith said. "Unless you're independently wealthy, you find any work that will sustain you."

What now sustains Smith is what he originally planned for: a career in education. After losing his seat in the House in 1990, Smith returned to academia as the dean of education and human development at The George Washington University in Washington. Though he holds a respected academic position, Smith explains that the transition, especially the pain of losing one of the most coveted jobs in the world in such a public manner, was immense.

"I left with pride and in shock," he said. "When you lose your job, facing unemployment is facing unemployment."

Smith's experience is stark in contrast to the image of former members of Congress wading through lucrative job offers from law firms, lobbying outfits, trade associations, and the like. While even one-term lawmakers aren't exactly a dime a dozen, their talents do not command top dollar in Washington's mercenary culture. Smith, as it turned out, landed outside the world of lawyers and lobbyists and assorted power-peddlers that's inhabited by so many ex-lawmakers.

In his disheveled office overlooking Foggy Bottom, Smith reflected on his voyage from his one term as Vermont's lone House's representative back to his family, profession, and private life.

As the founder and first president of the Community College of Vermont, Smith had combined his two avocations while serving in the Vermont legislature and as the state's lieutenant governor. With a doctorate in education from Harvard, Smith says that "I always had it in my mind that I would go back to education after I left politics."

But Smith was quick to find that being an ex-lawmaker isn't always an entree into a big private sector or university job. "Generally, former members are unemployed Americans," Smith said. "A lot of times, the first thing people do -- members who lose -- is getting employment which is commensurate with what they were doing." And that, he says, is often very, very hard to do.

Finding a job that provides the autonomy, prestige, salary, and perquisites that a member of Congress enjoys is more than a little difficult. What other occupation provides a staff devoted to solving every problem big and small, exemption from many fair labor and employment laws, exceptionally generous government benefits, police officers who stop traffic for hasty access to meetings, free parking places at local airports, and the knowledge that even the most mundane actions, such as answering a quorum call, are being recorded for history?

When Smith lost his reelection bid in 1990 to Independent Bernard Sanders, he tried to go back home to Vermont, where he still owns a home. But the winter of 1991 was not a good time to be unemployed, especially in the Northeast.

"It was the middle of a recession, a very tough economy situation back home in Vermont," Smith said. "There weren't really any jobs I was interested in that were available. I applied for jobs all over the country. I was very fortunate; within eight months, I was offered this deanship. I was very fortunate to find a job of this caliber in this circumstance.

"When I left Congress, my job search was in the area of education. My inclination was to go back to Vermont, but there was no work there. I think of it in many important regards as our home -- I still vote there." Like most Americans, Smith must live where the work is, and right now that job is still in Washington.

Smith is proud of his congressional service. He does not talk about gridlock or impossible schedules, but only of the honor of holding such an office. "It was the hardest work I've ever done," he said. "I enjoyed it enormously and I thought it was worthwhile. I have no empathy for people who leave government and then dump on it. Any important work is tough. Doesn't matter if you're a Senator, Representative, or a CEO."

Smith conceded, however, that congressional life is "a brutal way to earn a living."

Life today with his three children and wife, Sally, is drastically different from life during the political years. "It was extraordinarily exciting, and we reaped the benefits as a family," Smith said. "When you lose, it is unrequited love."

Smith tells a story of walking with his teenage son and breaking the news about the job at George Washington. The son put his arm around his dad and said, "That means we get to be a family again."

"It is safe to say my family still expects me to take on difficult assignments and not shy away from controversy," Smith said. "They are well relieved that that chapter of our lives is over."

Now the personal priorities are again in place. Sally Smith is involved with Habitat for Humanity and active in their church. They pay more attention to their kids' education. They no longer suffer from loss of privacy.

"The pattern is very different, being reintroduced to fatherhood, husband-hood, and privacy, Smith said. "There is a great deal that is very positive."

Located between the White House and the Georgetown section of Washington, George Washington University is a public institution with more than 25,000 students. Renamed by an act of Congress in 1904, it was founded as Columbian College in 1821.

"This school has upward trajectories," Smith said. "As a re-entry to higher education, an opportunity to work in a city, more than half-a-billion dollar budget, to be a part of the management team, that has been an extraordinary opportunity for me. I'm enjoying it enormously. I see my future in higher education. I've made a long-term commitment to George Washington to bring this school into the front ranks. Being offered this job was a dream come true. In reality, it happened a little sooner than I anticipated."

Smith's political nemesis came in an unlikely form. Bernard Sanders is a Brooklyn-born socialist who left New York City for the mountains of Vermont in 1968. Amassing a political cult following as the four-term mayor of Burlington, Sanders had come within four percentage points of beating Smith in the 1988 election.

During a debate Smith once pointed at Sanders and said: "The gentleman to my right is a genuine celebrity, a truly famous person. And there's a frustration [for me] in that." Smith said that even on Election Day, when he received only 40 percent of the vote, his polls showed that he had a 60 percent favorable rating.

Trapped in Washington during the final weeks of the campaign working on the 1990 budget crisis, Smith now blames two factors for his defeat: packaging and timing. "I'm a good retail politician, not a good wholesale politician," Smith said. "And I just couldn't get out there."

Smith also came under fire from gun owners because of his vote for restrictions on semiautomatic weapons. The bumper stickers read "Smith and Wesson, Yes. Peter Smith, No."

As the first Republican to endorse the doomed first budget compromise of 1990, Smith was also one of the few Republicans to support the next Democratic budget bill, angering many in his own party.

"From the beginning, I've viewed this as the first real opportunity in many years to fix a [deficit] problem that will inevitably cause us grievous economic damage," Smith told David Broder of *The Washington Post* in October 1990. "I determined that if I saw a package that was fair and enforceable, I would support it, even if I didn't like everything in it. I am not a power broker, so I have to take these packages as they come to me."

Back home, his position was helping to give Sanders's campaign momentum. "I think Mr. Smith was humiliated by the vote he cast that would have cut medicare $60 billion, boosted the tax on gasoline and home heating oil," Sanders said at the time. "Now he is trying to make amends."

Smith's campaign advertisements ended with the tag line: "Doing what's right isn't always easy. But it's always right." Trying to play on anti-Washington feelings, he told a group of senior citizens who were concerned about medicare cuts; "I'm surrounded down there by politicians who duck their responsibilities and postpone decisions. I'm not going to play that game."

In 1990, Sanders's huge personal popularity combined with political savvy propelled him to a 56 percent victory over Smith to become the first socialist congressman in more than 60 years.

"I was basically out there alone," Smith says of the budget battles of 1990. "It hurt me terribly when Bush subsequently said it was a mistake and raising taxes was a mistake. I believe he put the good of the country before his own political fate [with the first budget bill]. I have never understood the personal calculus in his mind that had him back off."

With increasing national interest in cutting the deficit, was Smith a statesman just a few years ahead of his time? "I don't know if I'm ahead of my time. I think they were worried about the economic stability of the country. It was conviction that led," he said.

"The farther away I get, I can see the difference between policy and politics," Smith said. "I take refuge from the fact that I've had an awful lot of people from both parties in Vermont and D.C. tell me I did a good job."

Will he ever run for another political office? "No, I don't really think so," Smith said. "I would never rule it out, but will I live my life in such a way that I will be available and be ready to run? The answer is no. It's time to move on.

"I'm over the ache (of losing). I'm proud of the positions I took and the work I did. Sure, I miss it. But it's a chapter in a longer story and it's over. It's a good chapter with a painful ending. I don't think about it much anymore. For us it was a lot of pain and a lot of anger, but we came to a point where I lost for reasons that I thought were important. That really takes a lot of the pain away. We did it for things that I believed in. For every door that closes, another opens."

The tale of "Peter Smith goes to Washington" was short, but it was full of difficult personal and political choices. "I left as a whole person," he said. "I had taken difficult positions I wanted to take on gun control, the deficit, civil rights. There were costs, but I refused to tailor my position to the political requirement. I left not having compromised my principles. I take away from that enormous pride. It was a great honor to serve in the institution."

In December 1994, Smith announced that as of January 1, 1995, he would be leaving George Washington University to become founding president of California State University at Monterey Bay.

The Revolving Door

For years, politicians of every stripe have been pledging to reform the way Washington does business. One of the easiest targets has been the revolving door between Capitol Hill and lobbying. Candidate Bill Clinton won rave reviews when he said, George Bush "won't break the stranglehold the special interests have on our election and the lobbyists have on our government, but I will." Campaign rhetoric aside, some former lawmakers seem to be destined to walk right back through that revolving door.

What is it that gives the revolving door such a magnetic pull for former Capitol Hill lawmakers. Money? Power? Prestige? Hard to say, though all three seem to be a common thread in the stories of Washington lawmakers-turned-lobbyists. In the case studies that follow, it's clear that former members of Congress who lobby their erstwhile colleagues can continue to shape federal policy and otherwise wield significant power. And while the grass isn't always greener on the outside, it usually is.

Lobbying provides a chance to retain the image of power and influence, reap handsome financial rewards for years of public service and possibly continue to be a player in legislative negotiations. The one-year ban on lawmakers lobbying their former committees has done little to prevent the exodus from the so-called 'money' committees to powerful Washington law and lobbying firms.

When Beryl Anthony (D., Ark.), Tom Downey (D., N.Y.), Marty Russo (D., Ill.), and Guy Vander Jagt (R., Mich.) lost their re-election bids in 1992, these members of the House Ways and Means Committee didn't lose any time becoming highly-paid health care lobbyists and dealing with their old committee and powerful friend, then-chairman Dan Rostenkowski (D., Ill.).

Ed Jenkins (D., Ga.) retired from the House in 1992 after 16 years, and his long time friendship with Rostenkowski paid off for his new lobbying firm, Winburn and Jenkins. "Rostenkowski usually seeks out Jenkins's opinion before making an important move," according to *1992 Politics in America*. Winburn and Jenkins represent the Health Insurance Association of America, Healthnet, the National Association of Urban Critical Access Hospitals, Pfizer Inc., Philip Morris, and Transitional Hospital Corporation.

The ranking Republican on the Ways and Means Subcommittee on Health, Bill Gradison (R., Ohio), won his 1992 race but then resigned from the House in

January 1993 to head the Health Insurance Association of America. Gradison, soon became the nation's most visible critic of the Clinton's health care reform plan. He even appeared in an HIAA commercial saying: "I'm Bill Gradison, president of the Health Insurance Association of America, the sponsor of Harry and Louise. Before taking this job, I served as a member of Congress from Ohio. I was the ranking member of the Ways and Means Health Subcommittee, so I know a little about health care and the Congress."

Ray McGrath (R., N.Y.) retired from the House in 1992 and now lobbies his former Ways and Means colleagues as the president of the Beer Institute. "A lot of the issues, whether it be excise taxes or advertising, fall within the jurisdiction of the Ways and Means Committee," McGrath told States News Service in 1993. "I know these issues and I know the players, so I can give a pretty fair perspective of what needs to be done."

Of the 99 former lawmakers in the study group who remained in Washington, 82 percent (81) became lobbyists. As a Representative, Michael Barnes (D., Md.) fought the Reagan Administration to keep the United States from intervening militarily in Central America. Later, as a lobbyist and foreign agent for Jean Bertrand-Aristide, Haiti's President, he networked around Capitol Hill to successfully advocate a U.S. military invasion of Haiti.

Howard Baker (R., Tenn.), the former Senate Majority Leader and Chief of Staff for President Ronald Reagan, is a senior partner in Baker, Worthington, Crossley, Stansberry & Woolf, a huge Washington-based law and lobbying firm. Baker has the resume of the stereotypical Washington powerbroker: a long legislative career followed by a stint as a presidential adviser, and then a name player in a lucrative lobbying business.

The firm also maintains an office in Huntsville, Tennessee, where Baker has a home. Baker's firm is a registered foreign agent for the Kingdom of Jordan. Its major clients have included EDS Corporation, Federal Express, International Business Machines Corporation, Occidental Petroleum Corporation, Pennzoil Corporation, Pillsbury Company, Pratt & Whitney, Ralston Purina/Brenmer Industries, Sprint Communications and United Technologies Corporation. Continuing their work with Baker are two of his former Senate aides, John C. Tuck and George Cranwell Montgomery, and former Tennessee Governor and 1996 Presidential hopeful Lamar Alexander.

Kent Hance (D, Tex.) gave up his House seat in 1984 to run for the Senate but lost in the Democratic primary. After a stint as the chairman of the Texas Railroad Commission (the state agency that regulates the energy industry), he formed Hance and Gamble, a law and lobbying firm based in Washington and Austin, Texas. "Started to go into pig farming but I didn't have enough money," Hance joked. "I wanted to upgrade. I'm living in Austin and do a lot of state and federal agency-type work. Business is good. When you leave Congress, you substantially increase your pay and substantially decrease your hours."

Bill Frenzel, a former Republican Representative from Minnesota, surprised many in Washington in 1993 when he went to work for the Clinton Administration as a lobbyist for the North American Free Trade Agreement. "They needed a Republican and they have chosen me," Frenzel explained at the time. To lobby for NAFTA, Frenzel took a leave of absence from his position as a guest scholar at the Brookings Institution and as a fellow of the Tax Foundation.

As the chairman of the Agriculture Subcommittee on Environment, Credit, and Rural Development Subcommittee, Representative Glenn English (D., Okla.) authored the 1993 revision of the rural electrical cooperative's federal subsidy program, which President Clinton signed into law in November 1993. A month later, English announced that he would resign from the House halfway through his tenth term to become the chief executive officer of the National Rural Electric Cooperative Association a position in which he lobbies officials who are directing the very legislation he wrote.

According to a former lawmaker, it is vital to former members-turned-lobbyists to maintain their level of influence, and sometimes that requires a "member-in-exile" existence. Even though he is now a Washington lobbyist, for example, former Representative Bill Alexander (D., Ark.) still has his business phone answered "Congressman Alexander's office." Others keep their flags, office furniture, and even staff members around. Business cards and letterheads are fashioned after official congressional materials.

Paula Hawkins, a one-term Republican Senator from Florida, uses her old title of "Senator" on the lobbying reports she files for her work on behalf of the Pharmaceutical Research and Manufacturers Association.

Washington watchdog groups have been sounding the warning bell. "We're at the point where special interests are running the show so much that there is a paralysis," said Pamela Gilbert, the director of Public Citizen's Congress Watch. "There is no leadership, no one willing to take the lead. The parties are blurring . . . Who's for what industry? That's where you get gridlock, and the average citizen is left out without the power."

Charles Lewis, the executive director of the Center for Public Integrity, agrees. "Things have gotten so incestuous inside Washington. There is a permanent ruling class, a permanent ruling elite that makes decisions affecting everyone. But the most elite are not elected. Officials are trading on their public positions and feathering their own nests. The lines becomes blurred between public and private."

Would further restrictions on former lawmakers resolve the debate over the revolving door? "Stronger laws don't solve the whole problem," said Nancy Watzman of Public Citizen's Congress Watch. "It's accountability. We need a heightened sensitivity to ethics."

"This town works to an extraordinary degree on human chemistry, who you know, who you trust," said David Gergen, a counselor to President Clinton and a former aide in the Ford and Reagan White Houses. "If you don't get that, you don't understand how this town works."

Bill Gradison

"I kid about this but truly I found that service in the House of Representatives is a fairly anonymous process," Bill Gradison said as he sat in his airy corner office in downtown Washington. "While people back home knew me and had certain expectations, other than the most senior and most powerful members of the House, members of the House tend to be a dime a dozen in this Beltway."

Certainly Gradison is no longer anonymous. After he left the House in January 1993 -- just two months after he won reelection with 70 percent of the vote -- he became the president of the Health Insurance Association of America.

From the vast HIAA headquarters, Gradison commands one of the most potent armies in the war over health care reform. Gradison's presence is especially felt in the House Ways and Means Committee, the site of key legislative struggles over reform and on which he carried a lot of weight as the ranking Republican on the Subcommittee on Health Care.

"I anticipated that the timing would not be well-received," Gradison said. "I didn't anticipate the spate of negative editorials from the morning newspaper back home. I still don't understand their position, but I have not exactly jumped around over the years. I've had two different political jobs in 30 years: Cincinnati City Council for 13 years or so and member of the House for 18 years or so."

"Ohioans of both parties certainly wish Gradison well as he becomes president of the Health Insurance Association of America," the *Cleveland Plain Dealer* said in an editorial. "Yet his departure could scarcely have come at a more awkward moment for the state's interests."

Local newspapers reported that some of his constituents weren't pleased with Gradison's change in plans. "He seemed to be the better choice at the time," one of them told the Associated Press. "Maybe he wasn't."

The HIAA made the offer to Gradison the day after he lost his bid to become secretary of the House Republican Conference Secretary. He was defeated by Representative Tom DeLay (R., Tex.), 95 to 71.

"We think he would be very effective in representing the HIAA," Ian Rolland, the HIAA chairman said at the time. "He brings a significant knowledge base. He is highly respected on Capitol Hill by both Republicans and Democrats. And he has the kind of stature to develop a program that reflects our concerns and keep the membership together."

Gradison is still defensive about the criticism. "Somebody told me recently, and I don't know if it is true or not, but somebody told me recently that the Senate Leader (George Mitchell) has been getting some negative comments back in Maine for the fact that he's leaving. I mean he's not doing like I did. He's not resigning during the term, but that he's not staying with that has obvious importance to his state and his service in the Senate. That's kind of what I caught. I don't think people were unhappy with me. I think they were happy back home. I think they were happy with what I was doing and would have been generally pleased had I stayed. And I had the safest district in Ohio. In the end, I ended up endorsing in a crowded primary, and the fellow I endorsed won and is doing a great job."

Gradison, classmate of George Bush at Yale University, continued his education at Harvard University, where he received a MBA in 1951. Work as an assistant undersecretary of the Treasury and as an assistant to the Secretary of Health, Education and Welfare in the Eisenhower Administration followed. After returning to Cincinnati to work as an investment broker, Gradison was elected to the city council in 1961 and played a significant role in the city's downtown redevelopment effort.

So why would this ambitious man, who had paid his political dues, and risen to a position of seniority in the House, suddenly quit? Gradison says that it was timing.

"I figured if I was going to make a change, I had to do it soon or because of my age people wouldn't think I was serious about taking on a demanding job," he said. "I got my medicare card last December, and yet I wasn't sure enough that there would be opportunities on the outside just to say I'm not going to run again. I agonized over that. I could envision because of my age -- 64 at that time or 63, whatever -- articles saying 'Gradison retires,' and I didn't see how the phone could ever ring again. I figured I'd be cutting the grass the rest of my life.

"So, maybe because I'm cautious by nature, I didn't want to compare something with nothing. I didn't want to compare leaving the House and not running again with maybe finding something else. It's regrettable, but it did happen after the election. I was approached about this position and made my choice accordingly."

For many who know him, it is hard to imagine a personality like Gradison forced into an unwelcome retirement, and the justification of resigning from elective office almost immediately after virtually coasting through a reelection led to some questioning of his motives.

"It has disturbed me that there have been totally unfounded assertions from some people back home that I knew about this ahead of time, which just simply isn't true," Gradison said. "And anybody who was involved in the search process can -- if they were just asked to show their calendars -- can document that. Perhaps that just reflects the high level of suspicion of public figures that somebody would think I've had a deal cooked up. In fact I knew there was a vacancy over here, and I had suggested several other people and then forgot about it. I never thought about myself."

"More people know Bill Gradison's name now than when he was in Congress," said Gilbert. "If he wanted people to know his name, he should go to Hollywood and become an actor. A number of people would give their right arm to be an anonymous member of Congress."

Lewis takes exception to Gradison's explanations. "First of all, the idea of a guy like Gradison mowing the grass the rest of his life is ludicrous," he said. "He knows a lot of people in this town, and all of these things strain credulity. He was a respected member. For a guy to be a member of Congress to cut out on their term and to become a lobbyist the next day is extraordinary. It makes people wonder how sincere you were."

The father of nine children, ages 43 to three, Gradison appears to be the same feisty guy who was renowned in the House for his intellect. He lives with his second wife, Heather, a former chairman of the Interstate Commerce Commission, and their four children. "I haven't slowed down a bit, but my life is somewhat more predictable in the sense that I have more control over my schedule," he said. "It's not governed by the election cycle or governed by the voting schedule of the House of Representatives. My hours at work are almost identical. I get up around 5:30 in the morning and stagger home around 6:30 at night. But at least I don't have night sessions and I don't have fund-raisers and participate in parades and things like that back home. I enjoyed doing that for 30-odd years, but I don't do it anymore."

The Clinton White House targeted the HIAA and its members for blocking health care reform in 1994, but Gradison defends his tactics, such as the now famous "Harry and Louise" television advertisements that the HIAA effectively ran nationwide and that helped to turn public opinion against Clinton's plan.

Hillary Clinton lashed out at the health industry, including the HIAA, in a speech she gave in November 1993. "They like being able to exclude people from coverage because the more they can exclude the more money they make," she said. "Now they have the gall to run TV ads . . . the very industry that has brought us to the brink of bankruptcy because of the way that they have financed health care."

Did the sudden intensity of the health care debate surprise Gradison? "When I left, I didn't expect that I or this association would be so visibly in the middle of the health insurance debate," he said. "We are and that's fine, but my style has always been to sit down and try to work problems out through negotiation. Once the White House declined to talk to us at a high level, then we had no choice but to develop a very visible advocacy effort, and that's what we've been doing. In that sense I am somewhat more visible -- a lot more visible. I have no desire to be visible, I just have a desire to prevail on the issues."

The chance to become a major player in a national debate would be a powerful incentive for almost any member of the House to reconsider his position. But Gradison said that it was the policy itself, not the power or the salary that tripled, that led him to resign his House seat. "One of my great personal desires has been to be involved in the development of national health care policy," he said. "And when I was approached to come over here, I thought I'd have a better chance to help shape national health care policy from outside rather than inside the House of Representatives.

"Had George Bush been reelected, I might not have felt that way, because I had personal access to him on health care issues. We had a good relationship going back over quite a number of years. In any event, from what transpired over the last year, I think so far that I made the right choice from a totally personal point of view. At the moment -- I say this with regret, but at the moment [summer, 1994] -- Republicans at the House of Representatives are on the outside looking in on health policy involvement, and the majority is attempting to pass legislation without Republican support. I do not fault Republicans or Democrats for that, that's just the situation. And my hunch is that if I had stayed there, as I would have as the ranking member of the Health Subcommittee, I might have been a very unhappy camper, a very frustrated member. I don't feel unhappy or frustrated right now."

Gradison's annual salary rocketed from $133,600 to a reported $395,000. But Gradison is a rich man in his own right. Gradison & Company, a family business founded more than 70 years ago, is Cincinnati's largest brokerage. The firm was acquired by McDonald & Company for $25 million in October 1991. Bill Gradison, as one of the two largest stockholders in Gradison & Co., then gained shares in McDonald & Company.

Two congressional aides joined Gradison at the HIAA: Chip Kahn who was the minority staff director of the Ways and Means Subcommittee on Health, and Bonnie Brown, who worked on Gradison's personal staff for most of his time in the House.

The one-year ban on lobbying by former members prevented Gradison from directly advocating HIAA's position to his former colleagues until February 1, 1994. But Gradison was in effect "lobbying" every time he was quoted.

"For a while I carried the statute around in my pocket, in fact, I think I still have it here, " Gradison joked. "I took it and put some plastic on either side and carried it around. I memorized the phrase: We're not permitted to contact a member of the House or Senate or their staff, quote, 'with the intent to influence official action,' closed quote. I remembered that, and I don't think there were any close calls. I bent over backwards to avoid anything that might even look inappropriate. Social contacts and things, I really avoided anything that might look wrong.

"Interestingly, the first day I was allowed to be up there was February 1st of this year [1994], and I was testifying with people from two other insurance organizations before the Senate Finance Committee. Toward the end of the hearing, two distinguished members of the United States Senate criticized our organization, and me particularly, for our television ads, and really gave it to us hard. And I took it, I hope, in good grace. Afterwards, I stepped out in the hall, and one of the networks was there and they observed what was going on, and in fact they used some of it on the news. They said 'Congressman, how do you feel about this one-year ban on lobbying by members of Congress?' And I said, 'I wish it had been five.'"

Rumors circulated around the Capitol that Gradison was violating the one-year limit and even appearing on the floor of the House. Gradison, however, denies any impropriety. "To the best of my knowledge, the only time I was on the floor of the House was for the swearing-in of my successor," Gradison said. "And I thought that that was appropriate. In fact, I cleared it ahead of time with the Speaker's office to make sure it wouldn't break any rules. I stood next to him, shook his hand, and left." You're not allowed on the floor of the House if the bill in which you have an interest is in mark-up.

"I think once, maybe they (the House) were in special orders, I once ducked in to use the phone. I don't think I saw any members. I walked by several staff and grabbed the telephone. I've avoided that, except for that swearing-in. I was very concerned when I started reading the rules over about the thought that I might never for the rest of my life be permitted on the floor of the House. I read the rules that way, but then on further inquiry it turned out that it wasn't quite that specific. But again, I was just trying to avoid an appearance of impropriety.

"It [the ban] wasn't a problem. I'm up there a fair amount now, but we've got a substantial federal lobbying staff in this organization. We also have consultants in this town and in both parties that assist us in lobbying. A number of our larger members have their own Washington offices, which work with us in coordination on lobbying. I'm much more involved in strategy than I am in lobbying as such. But I do try to get around there to visit with members of both houses and both parties."

In fact, Gradison had to postpone his first interview for this book because House Republican Leader Robert Michel had summoned him to Capitol Hill. Another summons to the Hill (which Gradison called his "daily health care crisis") almost postponed the second scheduled interview.

Leaving the House, even when resigning for what you believe to be a better job, is tough, according to Gradison. "I enjoyed my service there and I don't regret in any way those 18 years. It was a boyhood dream come true for me, literally. But I was ready to try something new. Maybe that's really what it comes down to -- maybe I was just restless. More than 30 years in elective office seemed about right for me. I've been telling my old friends from high school and college days that it's a good idea to change jobs every 30 years whether you need to or not. And that's kind of how I feel about it. I don't look back with regrets. My wife has said of me that once I make a decision I don't look back, not with just this decision but other lifetime decisions, and it's just how it is. I don't look back."

For Gradison, the tradeoff has been leaving his hometown of Cincinnati. But his four youngest children have always lived in the Washington area and now Northern Virginia is home. Behind his office desk is a large framed print of the old downtown area of Ohio's river city. "I've only been there (Cincinnati) once or twice . . . maybe two or three times at the most since I've started on this job. I had to give up my legal residence in Ohio on advice of counsel and become a Virginia citizen," Gradison said. "We had to put our condo up for sale back there. Gosh, it's been up for sale for six months and hasn't sold yet. We're basically trying to consolidate into Northern Virginia. I miss Cincinnati a lot; it's a great city. But there is no way I can do this job and be out there very often. Most of my travel involves visits with our own members of this association which are scattered all over the United States. So instead of going to Cincinnati, I'm going to Omaha, Hartford, New York, Dallas . . . all over the place."

Today, at age 64, Bill Gradison is starting out on a new career. He is finally getting his break at playing on the national scene. Having fun. "Some former members have told me they don't like to lobby. I love it," Gradison recently told a reporter.

Today, sitting in his downtown office, looking out over the capital's crowded business center Bill Gradison says, "I really haven't thought beyond this."

Tom Downey

With his one-year ban on lobbying barely over, Thomas J. Downey rushed back through the revolving door and signed on to lobby Congress for some of America's biggest and best-known corporations.

What makes this former New York Representative's new career so interesting is also what makes him so attractive to his new clients. His connections with the Clinton Administration, especially to Vice President Albert Gore Jr., run deep.

Downey has always been vocal about his friendship with powerful people. "The bitter irony about it is that my best friend just became the Vice President and I'm not going to be there to help in the next Congress," Downey told *The New York Times* the night of his 1992 defeat. "That's painful." It was Downey who invited Gore to play basketball in the House gym when Gore tore his Achilles' heel in August 1994.

Downey was also close to Dan Rostenkowski, the former chairman of the House Ways and Means Committee. "That's always helpful," Downey told *The Washington Post*. "You're taking your client to Morton's, and the chairman of the Ways and Means Committee comes over and puts his arm around you and says how great you are. That only has to happen once or twice and you're set."

It appears that Downey will be a player in Congress during the Clinton Administration and beyond. According to lobbying reports filed with the Clerk of the House, Downey and his lobbying firm, Downey Chandler, Inc., have been hired by Time Warner, Inc. for "all legislation affecting telecommunications and trade," by U.S. Healthcare and Medco Containment Services Inc. for "all legislation affecting health care reform, including the Health Security Act," and by Monitor Aerospace Corp. for "all legislation affecting defense conversion."

In addition, Downey's firm has been retained by both Metropolitan Life and Affiliated Companies and E.I. duPont de Nemours and Company for "all legislation affecting environment and health care, including the superfund reauthorization and Health Security Act," by the Breakthrough Technologies Institute for "all legislation affecting fuel cell technology and development," by Joseph E. Seagrams & Sons, Inc., for "all legislation affecting excise taxes and trade," and by United Feather and Down for "all legislation affecting H.R. 1741," which concerns duties tax issue on imported feathers.

A spokesman for Seagrams & Sons said that Downey is "working on a wide range of issues for us, obviously we value his experience."

Downey, a onetime liberal wunderkind, was elected to the House at the age of 25 as a member of the 1974 Watergate class. He made a name for himself as a leading critic of the arms race and defender of the environment. He was often mentioned as a future chairman of the Ways and Means Committee and even as a possible presidential candidate.

As a member of the House, Downey was the seventh-ranking Democrat on Ways and Means, the acting chairman of its Subcommittee on Human Resources and a member of its Subcommittee on Trade -- all assignments that Downey has capitalized on as a lobbyist.

"I am at the peak of my intellectual power and my ability to get things done," Downey was quoted as saying in March 1992. "I am in a position of enormous power in the House. The Majority Leader and Speaker are friends of mine. I can get things done. I am listened to. I have a lot more power than is generally understood on Long Island."

Yet Downey lost his 1992 reelection bid to Republican Rick Lazio after it was disclosed that he'd had $83,000 in overdrafts at the House bank, where his wife had once worked as auditor.

Downey was also featured in a 1990 expose by ABC News's Prime Time Live on a congressional junket to Barbados. As a hidden camera rolled, Downey allowed a former lawmaker-turned-lobbyist to rent a jet ski for him. The trip was paid for by taxpayers, and Downey and the other Capitol Hill lawmakers said they were on legitimate government business.

One of Downey's companions on the Barbados trip was Vincent P. Reusing, a lobbyist for Metropolitan Life Insurance and Affiliated Companies, one of the firms that Downey now represents.

When Downey moved to Capitol Hill years ago, his house became a social and political mecca for a small circle of Democratic lawmakers.

When Gore announced his "reinventing government" proposal in late 1993, Downey was there among the Clinton Cabinet officials. Downey told States News Service that he provided tips on how to market the proposal to Congress. At the announcement, Clinton did a double take. "He waved to me," Downey said. "He said 'Hi, Tom.' It was kind of funny."

Downey's post-defeat credentials received a huge boost in 1994 with his appointment to the Bipartisan Commission on Entitlement and Tax Reform, which was chaired by Senators Bob Kerrey (D-Neb.) and John Danforth (R-Mo.).

As a member of the commission, Downey continued to enjoy a "colleague" relationship with some of the most powerful lawmakers on Capitol Hill -- even as he was being paid to represent private interests. The 22 Senators and Representatives who served on the commission with Downey included such heavyweights as Sen. Daniel Patrick Moynihan (D-N.Y.), Sen. Alan Simpson (R-Wyo.), Sen. Pete Domenici (R-N.M.), Rep. Dan Rostenkowski (D-Ill.), Rep. John Dingell (D-Mich.), and Rep. Bill Archer (R-Texas). In addition the commission's members include the president of the United Mine Workers Union, the chairman and Chief Executive Officer of Salomon Brothers, Inc., and the chairman and Chief Executive Officer of Bank One Cleveland.

Even though a commission aide said that someone like Downey doesn't need a commission appointment to meet such people, because he has known them for years, the appointment doesn't sit well with public-interest groups.

"This is a commission with special-interest representatives on it," said Pamela Gilbert, the director of Public Citizen's Congress Watch. "But he is no longer an elected official representing the public. He is a private, special-interest lobbyist, and that should be fully disclosed and acknowledged. There is a big difference between when you've been elected by your constituents and working for a client. There are no more personal views. Who is going to be more important to Tom Downey as a lobbyist than Rostenkowski and Dingell? It's going to help Tom Downey tremendously. They [corporations] are hiring Gore and Rostenkowski's good buddy -- that's exactly who they're hiring. I'm sure his cachet is his relationships."

In addition to being a popular television news commentator, Downey also enjoys a weekly appearance on National Public Radio's Morning Edition, where he joins former Representative Vin Weber (R., Minn) for a discussion of current political events.

Richard Davis, producer of Crossfire, told *Legal Times* that "When we have Downey on, we don't know why he has the view he does, whether it is something that he believes in his heart or something that he says because he is paid for it."

With his lobbying career off and running, Downey has put his modest Capitol Hill home up for sale. At age 45, and with his elective political career behind him, it appears that he will be a powerful Washington force for a long time to come.

Beryl Anthony

When he lost his 1992 Democratic primary, Beryl Anthony was shocked. After serving 14 years in the House, however, he is making the most of his Arkansas political connections in Washington.

Anthony was the chairman of the Democratic Congressional Campaign Committee and a powerful member of the Ways and Means Committee. Probably most famous for his fund-raising prowess, he was popular with lobbyists as a pro-business Democrat. In his 1992 book, *The Lobbyists*, Jeffrey H. Birnbaum, a reporter for *The Wall Street Journal*, wrote: "Anthony had acquired a reputation on the Ways and Means Committee of being extremely close to lobbyists. Whenever a business lobbyist wanted a favor, he often thought of Beryl Anthony. And Anthony rarely said no. Lobbyists were an important part of Anthony's life-style. On many weekends he could be found crouching in a duck blind with some of Washington's biggest-name lobbyists."

Anthony's political troubles at home began in early 1992 when it was disclosed that he'd had 109 overdrafts at the House bank. Anthony is a member of a prominent family from southern Arkansas. He is married to Sheila Foster Anthony, whom President Clinton appointed to be assistant attorney general for legislative affairs. Sheila Anthony is the sister of the late deputy White House counsel, Vince Foster.

Anthony surprised no one when he joined the Washington office of Winston & Strawn, a Chicago-based law firm, as a partner and director of its legislation and regulatory practice. "Going through the interviewing process is much more emotionally wearing that I ever had anticipated," Anthony told *Legal Times* in January 1993. "I had a hard time making a decision. I had some very good competing offers." Winston & Strawn won Anthony because it offered him an equity partnership.

Winston and Strawn has since been hired by the American Hospital Association to lobby on health care issues and by the American Insurance Association. "Beryl Anthony knew the players in the Clinton White House and was Vince Foster's brother-in-law and we wanted insight on how the place worked," AHA vice president Richard Wade recently said. "This was a totally new set, with very few Washington insiders. Beryl Anthony knew them well. He was brought in to advise us, not to lobby."

According to lobbying reports filed with the Secretary of the Senate, Winston & Strawn also was hired by pharmaceutical manufacturers Pfizer, Inc. and Bristol Myers Squibb Co. to lobby in regard to tax issues, particularly section 936 of the Internal Revenue Service Code.

Section 936 provides tax subsidies for businesses with operations in Puerto Rico. Although Clinton opposed the measure, drug companies were successful in maintaining a reduced subsidy. Anthony has long been close to the pharmaceutical manufacturers and while in Congress raised large campaign contributions from the drug industry. In 1989, he was the chief sponsor of legislation that would have given tax breaks to drug companies for spending more on research in the United States.

Michael Barnes

When Michael Barnes decided to run for the Senate from Maryland in 1986, he gave up his House seat and a shot at becoming a major player in U.S. foreign policy. Barnes may have lost the Democratic primary to Barbara Mikulski, but his Washington career has taken off. He is now one of the most visible and highly paid foreign policy operatives in the United States.

Barnes, along with his Washington-based law firm, worked for Jean Bertrand-Aristide, then-exiled President of Haiti, and was the architect of the massive lobbying effort which resulted in pushing the Clinton Administration into a military takeover of the small island nation.

According to lobbying disclosure forms, Barnes and his firm, Hogan & Hartson, were paid a $55,000 a month fee in the last half of 1993 by Aristide, one of the highest monthly lobbying bills in Washington. In March 1994, they reportedly cut the monthly bill in half after criticism in the news media.

Barnes put together an immense lobbying effort based, in part, on his personal connections with several high-level foreign policy shapers. "I have tried to interpret Haitian reality to the international officials working on this," Barnes told *The Wall Street Journal* in November 1993.

As a member of the House from 1978 to 1986, Barnes gained a reputation as a savvy, liberal politician with an expertise in Latin American affairs. He enjoyed national prominence as a leading opponent of the Reagan Administration's policies in Latin America while he was the chairman of the Foreign Affairs Subcommittee on Western Hemisphere Affairs.

Barnes has remained active in Democratic circles. In 1992, he was the chairman of the Maryland Democratic Party's committee to coordinate local, state and presidential campaigns. He even accompanied then-candidate Clinton to a Baltimore Orioles baseball game in 1992.

Barnes's early political career included two years as a special assistant to former Sen. Edmund Muskie of Maine. Several years after Barnes left Muskie's office, Madeleine Albright, who is now the U.S. Permanent Representative to the United Nations, joined Muskie as his chief legislative assistant.

Barnes and Albright's paths eventually crossed at the Center for National Policy, a Democratic think tank. Albright was the Center's president from 1990 to 1993. Barnes, who had been an active member of the Center's board, succeeded Muskie as its chairman in June 1993. Muskie (himself now a registered foreign agent) serves as the center's chairman emeritus.

Government records do not indicate any official contact between Barnes and Albright regarding Haiti. But that is not true of Barnes and Samuel R. "Sandy" Berger, the deputy assistant to the President for national security affairs and one of Aristide's biggest boosters in the Clinton Administration.

Berger is a former partner at Hogan & Hartson, where he was a registered foreign agent and dealt in international trade issues. Before he joined the Clinton Administration, Berger played a major role in the Clinton-Gore campaign and transition team.

According to Foreign Agent Registration Act documents filed at the Justice Department, Barnes stays in regular contact with his reportedly close friend Berger, discussing "restoration of democratically elected government of Haiti."

Telephone logs filed under the registration law also show that Barnes had a telephone conversation with Vice President Gore about Aristide on February 25, 1993, and contacted Lawrence Pezzulo, who was then the State Department's adviser on Haiti, numerous times.

Barnes also contacted Vic Johnson, then the staff director of the Subcommittee on Western Hemisphere Affairs, regarding Aristide and testified before the subcommittee in July 1993. Johnson had previously worked for Barnes when he was the chairman of the subcommittee.

Even by Washington standards, the amount of money that Aristide paid for lobbying and legal services is staggering -- especially for such a poor nation. From February 23 to June 17, 1993, Justice Department records show, Barnes's firm (which at the time was another powerful Washington law firm, Arent, Fox, Kinter, Plotkin & Kahn) was paid $372,680 for "providing legal counsel regarding the restoration of the democratically elected government of Haiti."

Interestingly, before Clinton took office, Aristide's bills at Arent, Fox totaled only $42,000 for all of 1992, according to public records.

Barnes has said that his legal fees are "about half of what our bills for actual legal services would be worth if we were charging a corporate client." Hogan & Hartson normally charges clients $350 per hour for a partner's time, and Barnes has estimated that 10 lawyers at the firm spend time working on Haiti.

Barnes didn't become a U.S. Senator. But he became, what *The Wall Street Journal* called "a hired foreign minister for the Haitian government in exile." As Pamela Gilbert, a Washington observer, recently said, "Lobbying for war is a scary thing."

James McClure

Former Senator James McClure has continued his battle to save the mining industry billions of dollars by lobbying to protect the 1872 Mining Act from reform proposals under consideration in Congress.

As the preeminent mining lobbyists in Washington today, McClure and his firm represent some of the biggest and most powerful mining companies in the world, which currently mine federal land almost free of charge. In 1994, McClure, Gerard and Neuenschwander was not registered as a foreign agent at the Justice Department.

McClure, Gerard and Neuenschwander, Inc., represents 20 mining-industry clients, of which four of the largest - Kennecott Minerals Company, Placer Dome, and Minorco U.S.A. -- are owned or controlled by foreign interests. On September 19, 1994, McClure, Gerard and Neuenschwander registered as a foreign agent at the Justice Department. "They essentially represent a major percentage of North American gold production," said Tom Hilliard, senior policy analyst at the Mineral Policy Center.

As the ranking Republican on the Senate Energy and Natural Resources Committee until his retirement in 1990, McClure was successful in obstructing previous reform efforts. The Idaho Republican, a lawyer by trade, was elected to the House in 1966 and to the Senate in 1972, where he served three terms.

Within months of leaving the Senate, McClure founded the lobbying firm along with Jack Gerard, who had been his legislative director, and Tod Neuenschwander, who'd been his press secretary and chief of staff. McClure is also of counsel to the Boise law firm of Givens, Pursley and Huntley.

Gerard defended the firm's previous decision not to register as a foreign agent. "We represent the U.S. components of these companies," he said. "All have significant U.S. presence and are significant U.S. companies."

The Foreign Agent Registration Act can be ambiguous. "Just because they are foreign-owned does not make them liable to register," said Joe Clarkson of the Justice Department's FARA office.

According to the Mineral Policy Center's Hilliard, however, "If a company is chartered in Canada and their board of directors are Canadian, then that company is Canadian."

Signed into law by President Ulysses S. Grant, the 1872 Mining Act exempts companies that mine federal lands from paying royalties on the minerals they extract from those lands. In addition, mining companies are permitted to patent or purchase claims on federal lands for $5 or less per acre -- a fraction of the market rate. The estimated annual loss to American taxpayers runs into the billions of dollars.

A Senate-House conference committee began work in June 1994 to find a compromise on reforming the 1872 law. In the past year, the House and Senate each passed reform measures, with the House bill taking a much tougher stand against the mining industry by proposing to terminate the patenting process on public lands.

Royalty proposals range from the Senate's two percent to the House's eight percent. Oil, coal, and natural gas producers all pay the federal government 12.5 percent of gross for exploration and development on public lands.

Western Senators -- including McClure's successor in the Senate, Larry Craig -- have threatened filibusters if the conferees do not ease the patent and royalty provisions. The House bill would also require miners to meet federal environmental regulations, with the additional royalty money going into a cleanup fund for abandoned mines.

"Mining companies pay royalties to everyone else," Secretary of the Interior Bruce Babbitt said in May. "They pay royalties to the states, territories, private land owners, and to other mining companies -- everyone but Uncle Sam."

According to lobbying reports filed with the Clerk of the House, McClure's firm now represents Stillwater Mining Company, Santa Fe Pacific Gold Corporation, Placer Dome U.S., Inc., Phelps Dodge Corporation, Newmont Mining Corporation, Minorco, U.S.A., Magma Copper Company, Kennecott Minerals Company, Homestake Mining Co., Amax, Inc., Battle Mountain Gold, Brush Wellman Mining and Development Company, Inc., Coeur d'Alene Mines Corporation, Crown Butte Mines, Inc., Cyprus Amax Minerals Company, Echo Bay Mines Ltd., Euro-Nevada Mining Corporation, Franco-Nevada Mining Corporation Ltd., FMC Gold Company, and Hecla Mining Company.

Placer Dome paid just $955 for gold mining patent rights on federal lands in Cortez, Nevada. According to published estimates, its rights on that site alone are valued at $581 million.

Another of McClure's clients, Cyprus-Amax, paid $1,000 for molybdenum mining patent rights on federal land in Mount Emmons, Colorado. The estimated value of the rights on that site is a staggering $2.9 billion. The projected value of a Cyprus-Amax gold mine on federal land in Sleeper, Nevada is $600 million; the company paid the U.S. government $3,530 for the patent rights.

The firm's non-mining clients include World Cup USA 1994, Inc., Pacific Gas Transmission Company, The National Rifle Association, The National Endangered Species Act Reform Coalition, Idaho Power Company, and Cray Research, Inc. (for "legislation regarding supercomputing and acquisition of supercomputers by the federal government").

"The real interesting thing is that nobody is collecting those billions," Gerard said. "Those billions as suggested by them [mining reform proponents] do not exist. What will happen if they are successful in stopping mining on public lands is that there will be a loss to the U.S. of billions of dollars." In fact, he added it is the mining industry that is bringing forth the workable reform proposals.

"Senator McClure is certainly one of the most knowledgeable people around on public lands," Beverly Reece of the Mineral Policy Center said. "That firm is really the brains behind the campaign to stop mining reform, we've been told."

A Place in History: Dick Cheney

"Washington is full of people who worked in prior administrations and can't bring themselves to leave and spend the rest of their lives sitting around, with their nose pressed up to the windowpane, watching whoever's in power do it. Hoping that lightning will strike and they might conceivably be asked to go back into government again," Dick Cheney said. "And I find that's not a very healthy way to live.

"Wyoming has always been important to me; it's my home. It's beautiful country. I'm an avid fly fisherman and skier. I can do that much better in Jackson Hole than I can in the Virginia suburbs."

Dick Cheney is an old-fashioned kind of politician: hard working, hard-playing, straight to the point. A no-fluff kind of guy. His resume is tough to beat: aide to President Nixon, President Ford's White House chief of staff, U.S. Representative for 10 years, Secretary of Defense during the Persian Gulf war. A leader. A guy who wants to be in charge.

Cheney is a determined man. And today, his sights are set on the ultimate political score: the presidency.

Many professional political observers call Cheney the consummate professional politician. But they wonder whether he will be able to build enough popular political power without a clear regional or national base. Cheney has already been intensively travelling the country and raising money, speaking to all who will listen. Many do. This is the road, similar to the one Bill Clinton travelled, that the pundits predict Cheney will have to take if he is to be successful. Even after spending so much time inside Washington's power circles, Cheney in 1994, like Clinton in 1992, could be better off portraying himself as the outsider from Wyoming.

"I'm giving serious thought, myself, to whether or not I want to run for president in '96," Cheney said. "And I think that the place to do that from is outside of Washington. I don't think Washington is a legitimate sort of base to work from. You've got to leave the city to sort of reestablish your credentials in the country."

"I thought it was important when the Bush administration ended that I move back out home to the West," he explained. "My wife and I are both from Wyoming, so we bought a home in Jackson Hole, which is where we live now most of the time. We still have a house in Washington, but we're not in it more than one or two days a month."

But Cheney isn't in any one place for more than a day or two at a time these days. The quest for the presidency has turned into a multiyear process of speaking engagements and political chit- building. During this interview, he was traveling on a private plane from the Greenbrier resort in West Virginia, where he'd addressed the Chemical Manufacturers Association, to Orlando, Florida, for a weekend full of speeches. "I'm traveling a lot," Cheney said. "Been on the speaking circuit, the lecture circuit, for most of the last 18 months. Also, in addition to lectures to trade associations, business groups, academic institutions, and so forth, I've done a lot of political speaking on behalf of the Republican Party and on behalf of candidates all over the country. I've been in more than 40 states in the last 18 months and generally kept busy.

"What I did when I left the Pentagon was put together a package of several different things. I associated with the American Enterprise Institute as a senior fellow there. That's a Washington think tank that gives me a base of operations in Washington, a chance to do some things with AEI, and also refurbish my credentials in the domestic arena. Having spent four years on defense, I wanted to look at what's going on in the areas of education and crime and the economy and so forth. And you can do that sort of thing at AEI.

"So that takes a portion of my time. I've signed on with a number of companies. I'm a director of Morgan Stanley, the investment bank in New York. I'm also on the board of Procter & Gamble, U.S. West, and Union Pacific Railroad."

Cheney's journey through the highest levels of government began when he was a young graduate student from the University of Wisconsin doing a congressional fellowship in Washington. He so impressed his sponsor, Representative Bill Stieger of Wisconsin, that he abandoned his graduate studies to remain in Washington as a staff assistant in President Nixon's Office of Economic Opportunity. It was there that he worked for Donald Rumsfeld, who was the agency's director. When Rumsfeld was named to be President Ford's chief of staff in 1974, he took Cheney with him as a deputy. Cheney took over the top staff job the next year.

"When I was growing up in Wyoming, I was like most kids," Cheney recalled. "I didn't think of much except baseball, football, fishing, and girls. You know, it was a conventional sort of 1950s upbringing. But I did not start out with a lot of political ambition. I was president of my high school class when I was a senior in high school, that sort of thing."

Cheney is almost the accidental politician. "I really didn't think in terms of pursuing a political career," he said. "That came later. I really did start out to be an academic. Until after I was married and got involved in some internships -- the Wyoming Legislature, working for the Governor of Wisconsin as a congressional fellow -- those were the things that sort of took me away from the academic world into the real world of politics. And I discovered I really liked the real world of politics more than I did the academic world. So I ended up staying. Never went back to the academic world, but it was something that occurred after I was out of college. I was working on my graduate degrees."

The frantic pace of Cheney's early rise is staggering even by Washington standards. At age 34, as President Ford's chief of staff, he was working too hard, smoking too much, and too young for the job, he says today. Two years later, Ford lost the election and Cheney was out of a job.

"After the Ford Administration ended, when we lost the '76 election, I went back home to Wyoming and then ran for Congress in '78," Cheney said. "I just think it's much healthier than hanging around Washington as a has-been.

"I had some interesting propositions in Washington and some other big cities. I was 36 in 1977, when the Administration ended, and I really thought I might want to run for Congress some day. At that point there were no openings. If I was going to run for Congress, I knew I wanted to do it from Wyoming, which was home. And if that meant packing up your bags and going home to Wyoming and reestablishing your base -- your political base -- just was dumb luck that a few months after I got home in '77, the incumbent Teno Ronacalio, announced his retirement. Surprised everybody. Nobody knew he was going to hang it up. But he announced his retirement, and that created an opening.

"It was a little harried. I had to pass up alternatives to go and make a lot of money in the private sector or to stay in Washington or go home with limited economic prospects. And then, to bet the family jewels -- the savings -- on the question of a congressional campaign was a bit of a crapshoot. Turned out to be a good one. There was no guarantee at the time.

"Just because the kids were small, it was a real crapshoot, to pick up. I did not have a job in Wyoming; I had a couple of prospects. We literally took what savings we had, we loaded up a U-Haul truck, tied the car on the back end, and headed home to Wyoming.

"And it was not the economically smart thing to do. If I'd been concerned primarily about money -- I didn't have any money -- but if that had been a prime motivator, I would have stayed in Washington and accepted an expensive, high paying good job -- sort of bought into that. But I didn't want to do that."

Cheney felt that he had worked enough for other politicians. If he was going to remain in the game, better to be the front man than to stay behind-the-scenes. I had the feeling that if I was going to be involved in politics -- and I liked politics and government -- I wanted to be my own boss," Cheney said. "And the only way I could do that was to get elected -- put my own name on the ballot. So there was a strong incentive for me in '77 to pick up and go home to Wyoming for political reasons."

"When you're in a staff job, you're never yourself," he told *The Washington Post* in 1978. "It's humbling -- you're just somebody's hired gun, and even if that somebody happens to be the president of the United States, there's not much you can do on your own."

Once home in Wyoming, Cheney hit the campaign trail with the same focus that had catapulted him through the Washington staff stratosphere. "I announced my candidacy for Congress about November-December of '77 and ran a year-long campaign. Got elected in November of '78. Went right back to Washington as a congressman."

In fact, the campaign was not only an enormously draining experience for Cheney and his family, but it also turned out to be dangerous as well. Wyoming has only one congressional seat, so candidates must travel the entire sparsely populated state. Packing his family into a camper for the long, statewide drives around Wyoming, Cheney made the commitment to make the "crapshoot" work. In the general election, Cheney was to face a tough Democratic opponent, William Bagley, a deputy prosecutor in Cheyenne who attacked Cheney as a carpetbagger.

Smoking three packs of cigarettes a day and living on political adrenalin, Cheney lasted until June 18, 1978. Then, while he and wife, Lynne, were spending the night at the home of a friend while campaigning, his left arm started to tingle. He says that if it had not been for a relative who'd recently suffered a heart attack, he may not have given the problem proper attention. Once at the hospital, however, it became clear that Cheney, then 37, had suffered a heart attack.

He was ordered to rest for six weeks. The young politician came back a stronger, even more determined candidate. He formed a mythical campaign organization called "Cardiacs for Cheney" and wrote every Republican in the state a letter about his illness and how he'd given up smoking. "All of us -- Lynne, our two daughters, and myself -- like being involved in an effort which goes beyond our own personal interests," Cheney wrote. "Trying to achieve goals which benefit many people gives all of us a good feeling, an uplifting sense of purpose."

After the heart attack, some voters questioned Cheney's motives. Why would a husband and father of two young children risk his life for this? "Dick thinks it's important," Lynne Cheney told *The Washington Post* at the time. "Washington is the place where Dick can do something about the problems he cares about."

After he defeated Bagley, Cheney was back in Washington, but as a freshman lawmaker of the minority party, not in the high circles of power he had been accustomed to. But Cheney says that he didn't view it as a comedown.

"I was a congressman from a single-member state," he said. "Representing the entire state of Wyoming, I had exactly the same responsibilities in terms of geographic coverage that our two Senators did from Wyoming. And in Wyoming at least, maybe not elsewhere in the country, but at least in Wyoming among your friends and constituents, you were perceived almost on a par with your two Senators. I never had this sense of holding a lesser office because I was a House member instead of a Senator.

"I guess the other thing was, I'd been White House chief of staff already -- when I was 34 years old -- to the extent that there is a sort of stature associated with that. There is only one White House chief of staff at a time. I had already been that. It wasn't all that impressive, frankly. It wasn't all that it was cracked up to be, and I made a conscious decision that I wanted to go be a member of the House. Not out of any desire to attain a position of more stature, because most people say 'being a freshman congressman hasn't got the kind of clout associated with it that being White House chief of staff does.'

"I wanted to do it because it had that unique aspect to it of elective office. Put your name on the ballot. You go out and contest with others for the right to represent the voters of your district, to cast their vote on the floor of the House. And once you win it, it's all yours until somebody comes along to take it away from you.

"You don't work for anybody else. You represent the folks back home in the ballots of the Congress. I had a different perception, I think, of why I wanted to be a House member."

Things were changing in Washington during the late 1970s. Jimmy Carter brought in a new crew of outsiders to run things, ethics began to pop up more and more as a significant political issue, and Watergate was still a sore subject.

"My first term in Congress, I served on the Ethics Committee. John Rhodes, when I asked him just after I had been elected as a freshman, I called John -- he was then the Republican leader -- and said, 'John, I really need to be on the Interior Committee because that's vital to Wyoming and where all these public lands issues and so forth -- national parks -- and that's the most important committee assignment for me as a freshman.' He said 'Okay, you got it. Now, I want you to serve on the Ethics Committee.' The price of my going on Interior was that I had to be on the Standards of Official Conduct Committee. Ordinarily, they wouldn't put a freshman on that committee, but because I'd been around town before and already been at the White House and so forth, I was not a freshman in the traditional sense of the word. And so he asked me to go on and take the assignment, because he'd had difficulty getting anybody to do it.

"That was probably the most active period the Ethics Committee has ever had. And Abscam -- I spent a lot of hours as a freshman member of Congress watching my colleagues accept cash payoffs from Arab sheiks who were really undercover FBI agents. Those first two years I was in the House, I got a heavy dose of how not to do it and of all the problems that a lot of members had in terms of their ethical conduct."

Even after 20 years in national politics, Cheney has maintained his reputation as a 'clean' guy. When he was nominated to be Defense Secretary, the only dirt that could be found on Cheney were two drunk driving arrests in his youth and a fishing-out-of-season violation. "The $25 fine was not the worst part," Cheney said of the fishing escapade, according to Bob Woodward's book *The Commanders*. "They took my [expletive] fish."

"You always have to operate on the assumption that it's going to be an issue," Cheney says of ethics. "You just have to do business a certain way. You try to conduct yourself in a manner that's consistent with a basic set of standards in terms of what we expect in our public officials."

In 1983, Lynne and Dick Cheney published *Kings of the Hill*, in which they profiled eight of the most powerful House Speakers. "We got into the book, *Kings of the Hill*, because a publisher came to see me and said that they would like to publish a book if I'd like to write it," Cheney recalled. "And I think it was actually Paul Simon, who was then a Democratic House member from Illinois and a neighbor in the House Office Building, who had recommended that the publisher come see me. He had published a couple of books with the same outfit. The publisher raised the possibility of whether or not I was interested in doing a book. I implied that I was but that there were two requirements. One, I wanted to do it about the House, as we did with the *Kings of the Hill*. The idea for that really came from a chapter in Barbara Tuchman's book, *The Bell Tower* -- one of her great books. It was the period before World War I. She's got a chapter in there on Thomas Reed of Maine, who was maybe the greatest Speaker. And I was always impressed with what she had done with Reed, and convinced that there were a lot of stories like his. Men who had enormous impact at the time when they were in power, but had sort of been forgotten in terms of the national memory. They weren't presidents, so they didn't get the attention, perhaps, in the history books that all the presidents have, but they nonetheless had significant impact on the course of American history. So I wanted to do something like that.

"And the other requirement I had was that it had to be a joint venture with my wife, because she is the writer in the family. She's published several books, and is far more knowledgeable and disciplined about the profession of writing than I am. So we worked it out so that the two of us could do the book that we did. And we did the *Kings of the Hill*."

In their book, the Cheneys argued that recent Congresses have lacked strong leadership. "Today's Congress members find it extremely difficult to say no to interest groups that besiege them," they wrote in *Kings of the Hill*. "Political action committees and propaganda machines make it even more difficult for them than for their predecessors, and there is no strong leadership to ease the burden. The consequence has been all too often to say yes, yes to this group, yes to that group, yes to every group. The general interest of the nation is not served, for when the Congress gives all things to all people, the sure result is economic chaos for everyone.

"Power in the House will not be won easily, nor will its possessors find the responsibilities that come with it easy ones. Still, there will continue to be representatives who, loving the House and frustrated by it at the same time, will attempt to impose their will upon it."

Lynne Vincent and Dick Cheney were high-school sweethearts in Casper, Wyoming. They married in 1964 while he was an undergraduate student at the University of Wyoming. Cheney had begun his college career at Yale, but left during his sophomore year to return to Wyoming. In 1966, he received a master's degree in political science, and then both he and Lynne entered the Ph.D. program at the University of Wisconsin. Lynne finished her doctorate in English literature, while Cheney's formal academic career was sidelined after he entered politics. In Washington, she worked as a senior editor of the *Washingtonian* magazine.

President Ronald Reagan appointed Lynne to chair the National Endowment for the Humanities in 1986, and the Cheneys began to rival Bob and Elizabeth Dole as Washington's new Republican power couple. Today, Lynne Cheney also has an endowed chair at the American Enterprise Institute for Public Policy Research, where she is a Brady Fellow. In addition to serving on a number of corporate boards, she is in the process of writing a book for Simon and Schuster. "This is her third or fourth book now," Dick Cheney said. "So she's kept very busy. I haven't seen her in about ten days -- I'm in the middle of a 16-day road trip now. She's been busy, too. Our oldest daughter produced grandchild number one about four weeks ago, and Lynne's been heavily involved with our oldest daughter handling all of that.

"I started out as an academic. The reason I went to Washington originally in 1968 was to do work on my Ph.D. dissertation. I was a doctoral candidate at the University of Wisconsin and I had a congressional fellowship. That's how I got hooked up with Bill Steiger and Don Rumsfeld. And I had an interest in the House. My Ph.D. dissertation was going to be about voting in the House and the Senate, but especially the House of Representatives."

So how did Cheney, interviewed before the 1994 elections, see the House? "I think the House is held in lower regard today than used to be the case," he said. "A lot of that is the result of all the House members who spend their campaigns trashing the institution. I think it's a much more partisan place."

"My personal view, as a Republican, is that my friends on the Democratic side of the aisle would benefit from serving for a period of time in the minority party. It's been some 40 years now since there was a Republican Speaker. Basically, it's unhealthy for the institution. You've got all your committee chairmen on the Democratic side. With the possible exception of Jack Brooks, who was elected in 1952, I don't think there is a Democrat today serving in the House who ever served under a Republican Speaker. All your committee chairmen have always been in the majority. I know just from the time I was there from the late '70's until I left in 1989, the growing feeling on the part of the Republicans was that the quality of your ideas didn't matter anymore. All that mattered was whether you were a Republican, and if you were in fact viewed in those terms by the majority, they weren't much interested in what you had to say.

"All bills were debated on the floor under a closed rule. And if the Rules Committee would allow only a handful of amendments on any bill, they would specify what the contents of the amendments was and who would offer the amendments. And it became terribly frustrating as a Republican member of the House to serve.

As much as I loved being a congressman from Wyoming, ran successfully six times, when I was given the choice of staying in the House or going downtown and running the Defense Department for four years, it wasn't a close call. Partly because I felt I could have some significant impact for the Defense Department and I wasn't sure, as a member of the minority party in the House, that it mattered what I did.

"I think it's reached the point where we Republicans have become radicalized. There is a sense that one-party rule in the House, for such a long period of time, has just been corrupting and has contributed to the demise of the quality of the debate, the ability of people to get things done, and . . . the willingness of the institution to address the major problems of the day and come up with answers to those questions."

The House began to fall into certain political traps after Thomas P. O'Neill, one of the most powerful Speakers in recent years, left Congress in 1989, Cheney observed. "I served under Tip as a Speaker. Liked him, found him to be an honorable man. I felt that he extended me the same respect he did as anybody else as a member of the House. I'll also remember, for example, one day after we wrote *Kings of the Hill*, I was a junior member of the House, maybe in a second term. I'd sent the Speaker a copy of the book as a courtesy. He didn't know who I was, or I didn't think he knew who I was. And I was on the floor a couple of weeks after I'd sent him the book, and he sent a page over to get me and invited me up to the Speaker's chair. I'd never been invited to the Speaker's Chair before, never even been on the platform before. That was foreign territory for a Republican. But he invited me up and kept me up there for about half an hour for a conversation about the book.

"It was clear that he'd read the book -- he knew everything that was in it. Didn't agree with the way we'd treated certain people like Sam Rayburn, for example. He had some insights to offer with respect to Speaker Rayburn that were different than my view of Sam Rayburn, but they were fascinating.

"I always felt that Tip O'Neill was my Speaker. Even though I was a Republican and he was a Democrat. That disappeared with Jim Wright. When Jim Wright became Speaker, all of that changed. I don't want to attribute it only to Mr. Wright, but I think we lost some of the sense of being part of an institution and the ability to function on a bipartisan basis once we had the change in speakers."

There are a lot of different perceptions of Cheney's political views in circulation. He's a moderate. No, he's a Christian Coalition conservative speaking at the national convention along with Pat Robertson. Today, Cheney maintains that he has always been a conservative.

"I think there are a lot of folks in Washington who've never looked at my voting record, never done the basic research," Cheney said. "They say, 'Well he worked for Jerry Ford,' or 'He worked for George Bush,' or 'He's got a lot of friends who are Democrats,' and then make assumptions about my political philosophy based on relationships rather than looking at substantive votes. They can do it if they want, but they miss it if . . . it's more complicated than that.

"I generally have a conservative view of government, that government's role in the society ought to be limited. Ought to keep taxes as low as possible. Minimize the amount of regulations and red tape. And that government constitutes the biggest threat to our freedom, and that's the reason why we limited its authority when we set up the Constitution. Sometimes, some of my friends on the other side of the aisle lose sight of the importance of maintaining those limits. I have a different view of the world than the Clintons, for example. Part of it, I suppose, is affected by my early career, working in the antipoverty program in the Nixon Administration's Office of Economic Opportunity. We were working on wage and price controls. I came away from those experiences a great skeptic about the wisdom of an all-powerful government that has the authority to intervene, for example, in something such as the millions of economic transactions that take place in the country every day.

"You've got to let the market work. Wage and price controls were Richard Nixon's biggest policy disaster. That early experience left me with some strong feelings about the importance of recognizing that government could and should do some things, but not everything. Simply because you identify a problem in this society doesn't mean that there is -- or should be -- a government solution for that problem. I think I am, by that definition, a conservative."

Cheney displayed his political mettle when, at the end of his freshman term in the House, he ran for and won a leadership position as the chairman of the House Republican Policy Committee. In late 1988, he was elected the House Republican Whip, second in command to the Minority Leader Robert Michel. If Cheney had stayed in the House, he would now be in line to replace the retiring Michel.

Legislatively, Cheney looked after Wyoming as a House member in addition to building a solid national reputation on foreign policy. If I were to look at legislative accomplishment, I suppose it would be the Wyoming Wilderness Act that we passed in 1984," Cheney said. "We set aside about a million acres in additional wilderness in Wyoming. In terms of my committee work, I probably enjoyed the Intelligence Committee most and I think probably in terms of having an impact, made my biggest contributions there. But a lot of that was classified and I couldn't talk about it anyway.

"And the Intelligence Committee, because it operates behind closed doors, has a more bipartisan atmosphere to it. You don't get into the partisan wranglings that you do on the other committees. I think it was probably the highlight for me as a member of the House.

"Serving on the Iran-Contra Committee, investigating the Iran-contra operations, was a fascinating assignment. I don't know how productive it was, but it was fascinating. And I enjoyed very much being a part of the House Republican leadership. The thing that made my career more interesting, perhaps, was the fact that I got elected to the leadership at the end of my first term. But serving in that leadership for the next eight years that I was in the House, my aspirations were to follow Bob Michel as Republican Leader and I had that, I thought, pretty well wired. I had been elected Whip, the number two slot, without any opposition in late '88. Had just a few months before the President pulled me out. With Bob now retiring, if I'd stayed around, I'd have a good shot at the next Republican Leader. But that wasn't to be. I really enjoyed my time in the House, and I think a lot of what made it attractive to me were the extra things I was able to do with the leadership."

Cheney was not Bush's first choice to be Secretary of Defense. Former Senator John Tower's nomination had run into trouble, and Bush looked to Cheney as a safe choice that would win easy approval from the Senate.

As a high-profile Secretary of Defense, Cheney directed U.S. forces during the invasion of Panama, the Persian Gulf war, and the first relief efforts to Somalia. Today, Cheney says that the way the Gulf war was handled was "enormously important at the time, and a great deal of satisfaction went with it." Perhaps even more important in the long run, he says, is the way the United States presides over the end of the Cold War. The United States has to "develop a whole new military strategy, build a new force structure to implement it," he said. "Managing that change, that transition from the Cold War strategy and philosophy and approach to the post-Cold War period, was probably as important -- I'd put it up there as important -- as the Desert Storm, although it didn't receive nearly as much attention. In some respects, it probably has more lasting significance."

When 1992 rolled around and Bush lost the White House, the Cheneys were again faced with political unemployment. "When we came around to the end of that tour, we lost the election in '92, I immediately thought of 1976 in terms of picking up and going back home to Wyoming," Cheney said.

But Cheney is focusing again, just as he did after the Ford administration. He declined to run for the open Senate seat in Wyoming that was created by retirement of Republican Malcolm Wallop in 1994. "The main reason I didn't run for the Senate was because I really wanted to focus on the presidential contest, and I didn't believe I could do both," he said. "If I were seriously interested in looking at the presidency, I had to have the time to travel the country, and that was incompatible with running a Senate race in Wyoming this year. I felt I had to choose. I could not do both of the things well, and I didn't want to do either one of them poorly."

He is asked about what some Republicans believe would be the 1996 dream ticket: Dick Cheney-Colin Powell. "We've talked about that," he said. "The only problem is, we can't agree on who would be Number One and who would be Number Two," he told the *Cincinnati Enquirer*.

Last June, Cheney pleaded for party unity in a speech at the Virginia Republican Convention that nominated the controversial Iran-Contra figure Oliver North as the GOP Senate candidate.

Cheney says that for Republicans to win, they must stay loyal to the party, and that in Virginia, they should not have turned their backs on North. "The notion from the standpoint of the Republican Party of people can just pick up their baubles and go home," he said. "You can test for the nomination, you can run on the party's label, you run in the primary, and if it doesn't come out the way you want it to come out . . . so you turn your back on it and run as an independent. I guess that violates my sense of fairness and decency. It's also a double blow to our party. It's a guarantee for defeat."

The heart problem still follows him. He had quadruple bypass surgery in 1988, and now maintains a rigorous daily walking routine to keep himself in shape. In his wallet, Cheney carries a credit-card-sized printout of his EKG, just in case he should need it. During the summer of 1994, Cheney took a few days off the road to have arthroscopic surgery on his knees. "An old football injury," he said.

Back on the campaign trail, Cheney is working hard, but trying to take better care of himself this time. He takes a little time off now and then for some fishing, checks on the new granddaughter, and tries to decide if he really wants to run for President.

"Well, if I don't run for President, probably that will be the end of my political career, and I'll pursue other interests, presumably in the private sector," he said. "I'm still young enough at 53 to have other options, the ability to pursue another career. So one way to look at it is that I've had a great 25 years in Washington and in public life and enjoyed immensely my time in the Congress and as the President's chief of staff and as Secretary of Defense. But it's time to quit and move on to other things."

Off to another speech, another fund-raiser for the Republican Party, another step closer to his goal.

You Can't Go Home Again:
Bob Kastenmeier

"It was easier, literally, for me to get something here," Bob Kastenmeier said as he gazed out the cafeteria window overlooking Southeast Washington. "Going home for members sometimes poses a problem."

When the Wisconsin Democrat's 32 years in the House ended with his unexpected loss in 1990, Kastenmeier decided to stay in the same house in Arlington, Virginia, that he and his wife had built 25 years ago. The commute is still the same: over the bridge into Washington, and up to Capitol Hill. But now he drives past the entrance to the private House parking garage, past the Capitol, and continues one block to the Madison Building of the Library of Congress. In the small, bare carrel that the library has provided him, Kastenmeier can do his judicial research, write, or just plain sit and think.

Kastenmeier, who once found himself on President Nixon's enemies list, does not look like a menace to anyone. At age 70, dressed in a dark blue polyester suit, he looks more like the college professor or the small-town lawyer that he once was.

With almost his entire professional career spent in the same elective office, Kastenmeier had to make the unwelcome transition back to private life. "Half my life was spent in Congress," he said. "It was difficult. I served so long that I had to make many adjustments. But it was a great relief, and now I'm enjoying being out of Congress."

For all of his so-called radical views and crusades against the Vietnam and Persian Gulf wars, Kastenmeier is now concentrating on one of the issues he most fervently worked for during his 32 years in Congress: judicial reform.

Following his loss to Republican Scott Klug, Kastenmeier accepted an appointment as the chairman of the National Commission on Judicial Review. The commission was created by Congress in 1990 to make a report on judicial discipline and the judicial impeachment processes -- subjects Kastenmeier had devoted years to as the second-ranking member of the House Judiciary Committee.

Kastenmeier wrapped up his two years with the commission in late 1993, having completed the study. Now Kastenmeier supports himself on his government pension and a stipend from the Washington-based Governance Institute.

"I chose not to go into corporate law," he said. "It really becomes so commercial and very special-interest-oriented." While his years on the Judiciary Committee and expertise on copyright laws could have landed him a lucrative position with a Washington law firm, he says that he wasn't prepared to get back into a full-time job.

Money was never really what drove Bob Kastenmeier. Growing up during the Depression in some of the close-knit German and Scandinavian dairy farming communities in southern Wisconsin, Kastenmeier became a quiet, but powerful, legislator who rewrote some of the nation's laws and who was a thorn in the side of more than one President.

As the chairman of the Judiciary Subcommittee on Courts, Intellectual Property, and the Administration of Justice, Kastenmeier could have accepted hundreds of thousands of dollars in political action committee contributions. But he made a general rule against taking money from anyone with business before his subcommittee.

Just out of the University of Wisconsin's law school, Kastenmeier set up a law practice in the small village of Watertown, Wisconsin, in 1952. His entry into politics was his election as a justice of the peace in 1955. "When I first got interested in politics, I agreed to be the Jefferson County Democratic Party chairman," he said. "I had never planned to run, but in 1958, we had no candidate for Congress."

Once in the House, he became a liberal activist almost immediately. As the secretary to a group of House Democrats known as the Liberal Project in the late 1950s and early 1960s, Kastenmeier was a primary author of *The Liberal Papers*, a series of essays that the lawmakers published in an attempt to move the national Democratic Party further to the left. Kastenmeier says that he almost lost his 1962 reelection bid because of his support for then-radical issues, including the diplomatic recognition of China.

When the Vietnam war started heating up, Kastenmeier galvanized the opposition. "I followed my own conscience on this issue," he said. With the University of Wisconsin erupting almost daily with sometimes violent antiwar protests, Kastenmeier was put into a precarious position as a federal official. "I tried to find agreement with the students. I wrote to [Secretary of Defense Robert] McNamara very early on saying, 'What in the world are we doing being accomplices in something like this?' I had an early hearing on the war in my district in 1965, right after the teach-in. Arms control and disarmament issues concerned me. I remember telling people in the '60s that we had to go underground because thermonuclear war poses an absolute threat."

The Voting Rights Act of 1965 and the Civil Rights Acts of 1964 and 1968 were major legislative successes for Kastenmeier. "In the early 1960s, my efforts in the Judiciary Committee were directed to civil rights legislation," he said. "After civil rights ran its course, I think my contributions against the Vietnam war were most significant."

Kastenmeier, who was one of the few House members on President Nixon's enemies list, today says that he "never knew why" he was on it. But he was an active player in the Judiciary Committee's impeachment hearings. Kastenmeier convinced the committee to vote on the impeachment charges individually instead of collectively.

But it was the law and his almost anonymous work on the Judiciary Committee that Kastenmeier says he found most rewarding. He cites prison and legal-service issues, matters affecting the Supreme Court, and redistricting judicial circuits. "Things like that were extremely important to the judiciary," he said. "In 1976, the passing of the whole revision of the Copyright Act, which affects television, broadcasting, publishing, almost every form of communication -- the first revision since 1909 -- meant that this had enormous reach on what had transpired in the country."

Other significant accomplishments of his Judiciary Committee work included passing out of his subcommittee legislation that effectively eliminated the possibility of detention or concentration camps in the United States. And in a nation that's been held spellbound by the O.J. Simpson hearing and trial, it can thank or blame Kastenmeier, who fought for years to allow television cameras inside courtrooms.

The second district of Wisconsin includes the city of Madison and its surrounding suburbs and rural counties. As the home of the University of Wisconsin and the state capitol, Madison had long been a hotbed of liberal activism, and for many years Kastenmeier fit the political profile of the city perfectly. Today, the city has mellowed and has become quite prosperous with high-paying, white-collar jobs provided by an expanding corporate presence. But the changing politics of the city and the ever-conservative farming counties in the district made Kastenmeier's eventual defeat inevitable.

That opponent came in the form of young and handsome Scott Klug, a former television news anchorman in Madison, who attacked the length of Kastenmeier's congressional tenure. Klug started the "32 Club" (for Kastenmeier's 32 years in Washington), asking contributors to pay $32 to join. Klug's own pledge of serving no more than 12 years caught on with the voters and made him one of the nation's first successful term-limits candidates.

Kastenmeier also ran into trouble when he was one of just 29 House members to vote on October 1, 1990 -- just one month before the election -- against sending U.S. troops to the Persian Gulf.

"It wasn't just a matter of a single vote because I had made an issue of it out here," he told *The New York Times* in November 1990. "As one who voted for the Gulf of Tonkin resolution on Vietnam and always regretted it, I felt I had to speak up strongly this time."

Kastenmeier's campaign did not take Klug's "time for a change" message seriously and was completely surprised when Klug won 53 percent to 47 percent. "I suppose I must say I did not have an idea," Kastenmeier recalled. "Congress looked awfully bad in terms of the budget deal, and my opponent used correct strategy and was very effective at the end."

"It only cost me two years. I had told people that was my last race. My only reason to serve longer was to chair the Judiciary Committee, but that was not likely. I would have liked to have had two years without having to face an election. That's what I lost."

After the loss, accolades came from all over the nation's judiciary. "The federal judiciary really has suffered a great loss by his absence from future Congresses -- it's going to be hard to find someone to replace him," Joseph F. Weiss, Jr., a senior judge on the 3rd U.S. Court of Appeals, said after Kastenmeier's defeat. Even conservative Chief Justice William H. Rehnquist made a rare political statement, calling Kastenmeier "a good friend of the federal judiciary system."

Kastenmeier still believes that term limits would be "a very unwise thing to do, adding: "The unintended result would be to remove a lot of good people from office. Speaking as one who served 32 years, the third-longest in Wisconsin history, I've seen the various factors that cause people to come and go -- death, illness, loss, other offices, redistricting, or an unwillingness to serve anymore. Natural attrition for all these reasons causes sufficient turnover. I don't think it is constitutional for the states to impose on a federal election."

And today Kastenmeier is still toiling in his beloved field of law, working out of the nation's great library, working on Capitol Hill. "Issues down here [in Washington] I find more intriguing," he said. He would love to write a book about the history of the Judiciary Committee or his own political history but says that, at 70, his memory is starting to fade.

"It [congressional service] is a great job if you're interested in issues, if you want to express yourself and do something. It was a great experience, and I don't regret it. Thirty-two years is probably long enough to serve." Serving under eight Presidents, or something like that, you get a feel for political history."

Going Home Again: Lindy Boggs

"I love this city," Lindy Boggs said as a summer thunderstorm shook the magnolia leaves in the courtyard of her Bourbon Street mansion in the French Quarter of New Orleans.

Having just returned from a friend's birthday luncheon around the corner at Antoine's Restaurant, Boggs, at age 78, was resplendent in her hot-pink linen suit with heavy gold jewelry. With 50 years of Washington service behind her, Boggs now spends most of her time in the same district that both she and her late husband represented.

Boggs -- the name still inspires no small measure of reverence, or at least awe, in Washington. She helped to build a dynasty of sorts, and could leave the nation's capital secure in the knowledge that Boggses had made -- and were making -- a difference.

Lindy Boggs first went to Washington in 1940 as the 24-year-old bride of newly elected Representative Hale Boggs. He quickly rose through the ranks of the Democratic Party and was the House Majority Leader when his airplane disappeared in Alaska in 1972. After months of denying that Hale was dead, Lindy agreed to run for his House seat because it would be easier for her to give it up when he returned.

"In 1971, Hale was elected Majority Leader. It was widely assumed he would become Speaker of the House, but then his plane disappeared with Hale and three other men aboard," she told *People* magazine in 1990. "Carl Albert, who was Speaker of the House, called to tell me the plane was eight hours late. He didn't want me to hear it on the news. My first reaction was terrible shock and disbelief.

"The formal search went on until Thanksgiving. There were 55 investigations of sightings made during that time. I heard from a number of psychics all convinced that they were receiving information that needed to be investigated. The plane was never found. But even when I was finally persuaded to run for his seat, I'm not sure it was because I really accepted the fact he was gone. I figured that if anybody was willing to give up the seat to him if he came back, it would be me."

During her own 18 years in the House, Boggs also rose to prominence on her own as a bright and thoughtful leader on women's rights and numerous scientific issues. "I think it was Senator Bennett Johnston who said dealing with me was like Chinese water torture -- drip, drip, drip," she has said. The end of the Boggs era came in 1990 when Lindy retired, primarily to spend more time with her daughter, Barbara Boggs Sigmund, who was dying of cancer. Tragically, Sigmund, the popular mayor of Princeton, New Jersey, died in October 1990, two months before her mother's final term was over.

When Boggs left the House, the tributes were numerous. "In 25 years, I've never regretted someone leaving more than Lindy Boggs leaving this institution," House Speaker Thomas Foley said. "There is no finer lady, no finer member in this body than Lindy Boggs." The House voted to rename the Congresswomen's Reading Room in the Capitol "The Lindy Boggs Reading Room."

Today, Boggs lives in a largely hidden enclave on one of the world's most raucous streets, surrounded by T-shirt shops, open-air bars and children tap-dancing on the sidewalk with bottle caps stuck to the bottom of their sneakers.

"It never occurred to me that I wouldn't come home to live," she said as she sat in the second-floor sun room. "I've always assumed that when Hale's service in Congress was over, that we'd come home to live. As a matter of fact, the weekend before the hurricane Camille, we had settled on the plans and signed a contract to build a house on the Boggs property at Long Beach, Mississippi. We didn't expect to use it then except for the holidays.

"A month after Hale's disappearance, my aunt died and left me this house with the caveat that I not turn it into commercialism. So the only economically feasible thing I could do was to live in it."

A visitor arriving at the front gate of the home was greeted by a waiter from the open-air restaurant next door. "Is she expecting you?" he asked. "Sometimes that bell don't work. If you've got her phone number you can use this phone to call her. If she's expecting you."

Behind the plain wooden gate lies a private world that few tourists in New Orleans ever get the chance to view. The enormous rooms are decorated with French antiques and the ever visible courtyard serves as the house's focal point.

"The house has repaid me a thousand times for the decision," Boggs said. "It's a sort of a sorceress. I love being here, and I think I would miss it a great deal if I didn't stay for an extended period of time."

She has hosted many political as well as family events in her home, including a reception for George Bush at the 1988 Republican National Convention in New Orleans.

"New Orleans is a city of neighborhoods. It's very, very neighborhood oriented. When my aunt was thinking of moving here, my elder aunt called me and said 'you must speak to her'. And I said why should I speak to Aunt? She said 'because she's thinking of moving to the French Quarter. She was reared on Fourth and Coliseum!' (in the Garden District). The house is a sorceress, it makes you want to come back."

Life has not slowed down for Boggs. She maintains a busy schedule of personal and public engagements.

The week following this interview, Boggs was off to Tampa, where she served as the chairman of a conference on "Southern Women in Public Service," sponsored by the Stennis Center for Public Service, of which she is a director, and the Mississippi University for Women.

"I am on boards that have a continuing sort of interests of my congressional interests," she said. "I co-chair with Bob Tisch the Preservation of the Capitol Commission. I can still repair and beautify my glorious old building. I'm on the Folk Art Center at the Library of Congress. I was the author of the legislation setting up the Folk Art Center. I'm on the board of the National Archives Foundation, and I was for many years the member of the House who sat on the board of the National Archives. And I'm on the board of the National Garden, and that was also legislation that I introduced as part of the Bicentennial of the Congress. I'm on the board of the Georgetown Law Center, and that keeps me very interested. I have a nice little office and a wonderful title. I'm the special counsel to the president of Tulane University."

Still active in Democratic national politics, she was one of the founders of the Democratic Leadership Council. "I'm some officer," she joked. "I know that I sign checks occasionally."

Her son, Washington superlobbyist Thomas Hale Boggs, Jr., and daughter, ABC-TV and National Public Radio correspondent Cokie Roberts, still live in Washington and are major-league players in today's political scene.

The telephone in Boggs's home seems to never stop ringing. This time a New Orleans acquaintance is calling to ask for advice on how to contact a ranking Senator. When asked about maintaining her influence in Washington, she responded by giggling and saying, "If you do remain influential, it's because you keep asking."

"When you're a sitting member, people are always very respectful of your time and the lack of time that you usually have," she said. "After you're retired, it doesn't occur to them that you don't have all the time in the world. And when they call you they will immediately start talking on the telephone about the problem they wish to address or the information they wish to share or whatever it is without ever once saying, 'Do you have time?, 'Am I interrupting you?,' or 'How much time do you have?' They just launch into whatever it is they called you about no matter how complicated it may be."

Hale Boggs was a reform-minded Louisiana Democrat just three years out of Tulane Law School when he was elected to the House at 26. During the first election, the Boggses forged a political partnership that would continue through their married life. "I was always designated as a coordinator because nobody could manage Hale Boggs," Lindy Boggs explained, her blue eyes drifting. "I'd always worked real hard, and we lived next door to my elder aunt in the Garden District, where we both had huge dining-room tables. All the volunteers came to both houses to work in the campaign. The factions within Hale's congressional district, the Democratic factions, were such that they argued with each other, and any campaign manager he could have selected would have to belong to one or the other of these factions which would have been difficult for the other factions to swallow. So I sort of came upon the job as a coordinator so that I could be accepted by all the factions. Once that occurs, of course, you never get rid of the position."

Once in Washington, the young Lindy Boggs had to get used to the ways of the Capitol. "The mother of one of my good friends told me when I was going to Washington: 'Dear, the most sophisticated and becoming thing a woman can wear is a purple veil. If you ever need that knowledge, just remember it.'

"So, Hale was on Banking and Currency, and that is where lend-lease legislation was. We were a generation of isolationists. Franklin Roosevelt had just campaigned on 'I will not send your sons to war.' It was 'America First' and all those things. We woke up at Pearl Harbor, but before then it was difficult to move the Congress in the direction of the people who became our allies. Hale called me and said: 'you really should come down to these hearings. You need to know the serious situation that exists. Come on down to such-and-such a room in such-and-such a building.'

"I had two babies, of course, but thank heavens I had a nurse. But I had on a sweater and skirt and loafers. So I put on high heels, put on a blazer, put on some earrings. I dashed down to the Capitol. In those days you didn't have a picture on anything. There was this long line of people waiting to get into the hearing room, and I sort of wormed my way up to the clerk at the door and said, 'My husband is a member of the committee and he's asked me to come down to the hearing.' And he said, 'Oh, sure.'

"So I went home and put on my black Davidow suit, and my pearl circle pin, and my white gloves, and my black velour hat. And I went to the store near the Capitol called Palais Royal, where I had opened an account because I needed a baby bed the first day I was there. I went up to the veil and glove counter and asked this lady to drape a purple veil on my hat. She was thrilled, and she did, and I went strutting back to the Capitol. I went up to the guard and said: 'I'm Mrs. Boggs. I'd like to be seated, please.' 'Oh, yes ma'am,' he said.

"The only way to see Washington is through a purple veil," she said with a smile. This is such a telling Washington story that Boggs has titled her autobiography, *Washington Through a Purple Veil.*

Much has changed in the House since Lindy and Hale Boggs first went to Washington. Because Congress wasn't in session from September through January, congressional families could stay in their districts for four months out of the year. The current full-time nature of Congress and the lack of sociability bothers Boggs.

"You know how lawyers will argue a case in court and then go out to lunch together," she said. "Oftentimes, over the weekends, particularly when the weather was clear, people would have cookouts and other people would come over. Somebody had been on a hunting trip, and everybody on the trip had given them their ducks or their quail or whatever. And it was very social."

The Boggses were always social leaders in Washington. They were young, attractive, and just plain fun. It was a combination that could also advance a young political career. "When Hale first joined the Ways and Means Committee, Mr. O'Brien from Chicago was on the committee. Charlie Davis was the chief counsel of the committee, and Charlie was from Chicago as well. And the Davises and the Boggses became very good friends, and Jean and I are still very good friends.

"When Mr. O'Brien was 80, Hale and Charlie decided to give him a birthday party. And Mr. O'Brien was thrilled with the idea and kept adding people to invite, and adding people to invite and we ended up with about 1,000 people. We thought it was a grand occasion for his 80th birthday, right? The next year he started, 'You know, it's only three months till my birthday.' So for five years we gave Mr. O'Brien a birthday party out at the house in Bethesda.

"It was always that big, and it was a wonderful party because you had the Congress, and the staff members, and the press, and the White House people, and the Cabinet people, and usually the President would drop by for a minute. And everybody got to see each other at a social setting, which was unusual to have everybody together. Of course, it was very popular. And when Mr. O'Brien left Congress after his 85th birthday, people began to call us the next year and say: 'Are we off your list? What did we do to get off your list?' They didn't remember that it was in honor of Mr. O'Brien at all. We gave those doggone parties for 15 years until Hale went off to the wild blue yonder. Charlie retired to a good law firm in Chicago, and he had to come back to give the parties."

Despite the glamour and celebrity that went along with being a lawmaker's wife in Washington, there was the reality of raising children in two different states. "One of the real problems was carpooling children to school. Because many of us lived at home during the "R" months and came back to Washington for January, and you were out of the loop for carpools," she recalled. "Often we got together, the congressional mothers, got together to carpool and it was a big family. A very sociable family.

"No matter how hard you may fight on the floor or in committee, when you were out together as good friends and family members, all that was put aside. Oftentimes you could work out good compromises. You understood where people were coming from, what their limitations were according to the congressional districts that they had to represent.

"I think there was more personal respect among the members. I don't mean that there weren't rivalries. Of course there were. There was really much more comraderie. And that was one of the aspects of the service that made it compatible with happy living. And I think it made people more satisfied with their service than they are now. So often, people are compelled to render the service and yet they feel almost angry about it. And I don't understand why with TV, and faxes, and E-mail and so on that people need to go home as much as they do."

Boggs believes that Congress was more effective before airline travel made returning home every weekend the norm. Today, with most legislative work-weeks lasting only three days, it is easy to see why last-minute extended sessions are often necessary.

"Almost every month there is some national occasion that allows you to go home over an extended weekend," she said. "If there is a compelling reason to go to some big event or something, that would be another reason to go home. But to feel that you have to go home every weekend. And that means you want to leave Friday afternoon so you don't get much done on Friday. That means you want to stay over Monday, so you don't get back until Tuesday. The legislative session lags because it only has three days of hard-hitting session. I think that's unfortu-nate. It's hard on everyone's family life. It's hard on staff members. Keep them in Washington the whole week so that they can do their business."

When Boggs speaks fondly of the years of service, it is of policy accomplish-ments. There is no mention of the Kennedy and Johnson inaugural balls she chaired or of the family weddings with Presidents in attendance. Her emphasis is on the battles won, both large and small, as a Southern woman persevering in a man's world. "I went from being president of everything to being a mere member of Congress," she once told a reporter.

It is the policy that enthralls her today, not the politics. And somewhat unex-pectedly, it was women's issues that involved a big part of her congressional career. "I think that there were probably several steps in promoting women's issues that were gratifying," she said. "I always found that it was more or less being a woman in the right place at the right time. When I went to Congress there were 16 women members, and I was the first woman to be elected to the House from Louisiana. I didn't even realize that when I was running. I was running to continue Hale's work. So I suppose what I'm saying is I didn't run as a feminist, but I was able to be in the right place at the right time. I was able to promote the causes and fairness in housing, insurance and health care, education, equal opportunities in government work and government contracts.

"I was so amused because Cokie's daughter, Rebecca, after she graduated from Princeton, was working in a Western women's shelter doing her good deeds for a year. She called me one day and said: 'Mama, thank you so much for insisting that women and minorities be included in government contracts. I placed nine women in construction today.' "

Again the policy dominates the memory. "The object was to have women trained in jobs that were not usual women's jobs because they were better paying jobs so they could get off welfare," she explained. "Being trained and being able to get jobs that paid them enough to stay off welfare and still get their children's health benefits and food."

After Hale's death, Lindy had to deal with a number of issues on her own, including finances. When she had trouble getting credit as a single woman to buy her Washington condo, she did something about it.

"Banking and Currency, the financial institutions subcommittee, was redoing a mortgage lending aspect of the Banking Act," she said. "And there was an amendment that said there could be no discrimination due to race or age or veterans status. I just ran over to the side room and cranked out 47 pages that said 'no sex or marital status,' and that's how it got into the law.

"Oh, I came back in and put on my best Southern airs and said, 'knowing the composition of this committee, I realize this is just an oversight, however.' So it got accepted and stayed in the House bill, and then the Senate accepted it in conference. But if I hadn't been there, if I hadn't been a woman in the subcommittee meeting helping to mark up a bill? It would have occurred to me, but would it have occurred to them?"

Scientific advances also interested Boggs and as a member of the Appropriations Committee, she was able to help finance a number of historic projects. "Because I was on the Appropriations subcommittee that dealt with great scientific debates, I used to say that I felt like Elizabeth and Isabella," she said. "I was willing to give my country's fortune to the exploratory missions. I was on NASA and the National Science Foundation, the Federal Emergency Management Agency, and almost all the scientific explorations and exploratory missions. I suppose involvement in scientific achievements would be one of the most important contributions I was able to make legislatively."

As a natural conciliator, Boggs sometimes struggled with voting. While debating an issue during a panel discussion Cokie Roberts recently said, "Being my mother's daughter, I agree with both of you."

"The hardest thing, of course, was that you had to vote, and there was no 'maybe' button," Boggs said. "That meant you had to disappoint people . . . choose among friends, choose among good proposals, and that was hard because I'd always been a conciliator. I'd smooth people's feelings when Hale had to vote."

The decision to leave the House, after 50 years of combined service, was painful, though not nearly as painful as the personal tragedy that prompted the move.

Barbara Boggs Sigmund lost her left eye to cancer in 1982. Known as flamboyant, bright, and funny, she was elected mayor of Princeton, but ran unsuccessful campaigns for Senator and Governor. She made her colorful eyepatches her trademark even distributing eyepatches to supporters as a campaign gimmick.

"Mother cannot accept the fact that I may die before she does -- it's not in the natural order of things," Sigmund said in a 1990 interview. "When I lost my eye in 1982, we felt it was a case of 'If thine eye offend thee, pluck it out' and that was the end of it. So learning that the cancer had spread was traumatic. The worst part was telling Mother. She said, 'I wish I could rock you and make it all better.'

Such a Mama thing to say."

"I had not planned on Barbara's death this soon, and I will look at things differently," Boggs told States News Service in November 1990. During the interview for this book, when she mentioned her daughter Barbara's name, tears began to gently fall on her cheeks, though her voice was unfailing.

"I think it would have been very hard if I hadn't been so involved in all these committees that I had been asked to join," she said quietly. "It was time to leave. So many of the things that we had worked for had seemed to come true. We thought the Cold War was over, and looking as we had elected a Democratic President ahead of us. Many of the programs I'd worked on, Hale had worked on, here at home had come to fruition. A good many of the programs that I had helped with the appropriations were in place. So it seemed an appropriate time to leave."

Directory

Senator James Abdnor (R., South Dakota)

Abdnor was elected to the House in 1972 and then elected to the Senate in 1980. In 1986, he lost his reelection bid to Democrat Tom Daschle. Appointed by President Reagan to head the Small Business Administration in 1986, Abdnor returned home to his ranch in South Dakota in 1988. In 1992, he was appointed to a three-year term on the National Public Lands Advisory Council by Interior Secretary Manuel Lujan.

Abdnor used approximately $8,700 in leftover campaign funds to pay for travel, telephone, storage fees, and other expenses. He contributed $6,125 to other political candidates and gave $22,500 to the South Dakota State Historical Society. Abdnor has $34,820 left in his campaign fund.

Home Address
P.O. Box 217
Kennebec, South Dakota 57544
(605) 343-6387 or (605) 343-6387

Representative Neil Abercrombie (D., Hawaii)

Abercrombie was elected to the House in a special election on September 20, 1986 to fill the seat vacated by Cecil Heftel. He lost the 1986 general election just weeks later.

A former preschool custodian, a probation officer, and a college teaching assistant, Abercrombie was a radical activist during the 1960s. In a political comeback in 1990, he was elected to the House, where he currently serves.

Business Address
1440 Longworth House Office Building
Washington, D.C. 20510
(202) 225-2776

Senator Brock Adams (D., Washington)

Adams was elected to the House in 1964, where he served until 1977. President Jimmy Carter appointed him Secretary of Transportation in 1977. In 1986, Adams narrowly defeated Republican Senator Slade Gorton. He served one term before he was forced to retire in 1992 amid accusations of sexual misconduct.

Adams abandoned his reelection campaign on March 1, 1992, the same day *The Seattle Times* reported that he had allegedly sexually abused eight women. Kari Tupper, a family friend and congressional aide, claimed that Adams had drugged and molested her in his Washington home.

"This is the saddest day of my life," Adams said as he announced the end of his candidacy. "I care for people and I have never harmed anyone. But I find now that it is not worth it to continue this campaign."

Adams is now retired and living in Maryland.

Home Address
138 Tanner's Point Road
Cove Creek Club
Stevensville, Maryland 21666
(410) 643-2558

Representative Joseph Addabbo (D., New York)

Addabbo, who was elected to the House in 1960, died in office on April 10, 1986. Addabbo's estate received $145,118 in leftover campaign funds.

Senator Daniel Akaka (D., Hawaii)

Akaka was elected to the House in 1976, where he served until his appointment in 1990 to fill the Senate seat left vacant by the death of Spark Matsunaga. He defeated Representative Patricia Saiki in a 1990 special election and currently serves in the Senate.

Business Address
720 Hart Senate Office Building
Washington, D.C. 20515
(202) 224-2361

Representative Donald Albosta (D., Michigan)

Albosta, who was elected to the House in 1978, lost his seat in the 1984 election to Republican Bill Schuette by 1,314 votes. He is now a farmer and businessman in Michigan.

Business Address
4400 Fry Road
St. Charles, Michigan 48655
(517) 770-4234

Representative William Alexander (D., Arkansas)

Alexander was elected to the House in 1968. He lost the 1992 Democratic primary to his former congressional aide, Blanche Lambert, after it was disclosed that he had 487 overdrafts at the House bank during a three-year period.

After his defeat, Alexander sold his Capitol Hill townhouse and moved to the Washington suburb of McLean, Virginia. In 1993, he joined the Washington-based law firm of McAuliffe, Kelley & Rafaelli. He left the firm in 1994 to start his own lobbying firm, Alexander & Associates. Judy Smith, his former congressional assistant, has stayed with Alexander and now answers the telephone at the lobbying firm "Congressman Alexander's office." Alexander is a registered foreign agent.

Alexander says that his business "represents individuals, corporations, and public entities in state and federal courts and before government agencies, including committees of the Congress. Also commercial and business transactions."

"Congress mirrors the images of a nation of people in search of their destiny," Alexander told us. Thus, Congress is a confluence of the economic, social, and political forces that ultimately forge national policy. It is a rare privilege to have learned how democracy works."

Business Address
Alexander & Associates
1425 Ironwood Drive
McLean, Virginia 22101
(202) 628-5914

Home Address
1425 Ironwood Drive
McLean, Virginia 22101
(703) 533-0058

Representative George Allen (R., Virginia)

Allen was elected to the House in a special election in 1991 to fill the seat left vacant by the resignation of Representative D. French Slaughter for health reasons. He retired in 1992 after what he called "vicious partisan gerrymandering."

"The new 7th District was drawn to include my home and the home of Representative Tom Bliley, with nearly 70 percent of Tom's current district," Allen wrote in *Roll Call* in 1992. "Clearly I could not run in this district, nor would I have run against Tom, whom I greatly respect and admire."

He was elected governor of Virginia in 1993. "My short term in the U.S. House of Representatives taught me much about Washington, D.C., and it certainly affirmed my belief that the federal government, and Congress in particular, is overreaching and oppressive," Allen told us. "As outlined in the Constitution, states have certain rights not under the domain of the federal government, and it is now my duty as governor to defend those rights."

Business Address	*Home Address*
Office of the Governor	R.F.D. 1, Box 214
State Capitol	Earlysville, Virginia 22936
Richmond, Virginia 23219	
(804) 786-2211	

Representative Glenn Anderson (D., California)

Anderson was elected to the House in 1978. He retired in 1992, at age 79, to run his family's property management firm. In 1990, his colleagues stripped him of his chairmanship of the Public Works and Transportation Committee citing ineffectiveness. Anderson's stepson, Evan Braude Anderson, lost his 1992 attempt to succeed him in Congress.

Business Address
11918 Hawthorne Boulevard
Hawthorne, California 90250
(310) 973-7343

Representative Ike Andrews (D., North Carolina)

Andrews was elected to the House in 1972, but lost the 1984 election to Republican Bill Cobey. "I'm practicing law in my old hometown, Siler City, where I began," he told us. I'm having a good time and trying to re-learn a little bit about golf and getting to know my grandchildren, who spend most every weekend with us."

Business Address	*Home Address*
Edwards, Atwater & Andrews	138 Fearington Post
P.O. Box 629	Pittsboro, North Carolina 27312
Siler City, North Carolina 27344	(919) 542-0528
(919) 663-2850	

Senator Mark Andrews (R., North Dakota)

Andrews was elected to the House in a special election in October 1963. He won his 1980 Senate race but served just one term, losing in 1986 to Democrat Kent Conrad. After he left the Senate, he formed Andrews & Associates, a Washington lobbying firm.

Andrews told us that working on issues for clients is no different than working on issues for constituents. "That (Congress) was interesting and this (lobbying) is interesting." He also says that his job as a lobbyist is not to gain access for his clients but to make the issues they support "more compelling."

Although he now lives and works in Washington, Andrews says that he frequently gets back to his farm in North Dakota and serves on several boards of directors in the state.

Business Address	*Home Address*
2550 M Street, N.W., #450	2500 Virginia Ave., N.W.
Washington, D.C. 20037	Washington, D.C. 20037
(202) 457-5671	(202) 338-6148

Representative Frank Annunzio (D., Illinois)

Annunzio was elected to the House in 1964, where he served until his retirement in 1992. He retired after a redistricting battle threw him into the same district as Representative Dan Rostenkowski. As the chairman of the powerful Banking and Financial Institutions Subcommittee, Annunzio was investigated in 1989 and 1990 for his close relationship to the savings and loan industry and Charles Keating.

Annunzio returned to Chicago after leaving office and in 1993, he was appointed to a five-year term on the Illinois International Post District Board.

Business Address
Legislative Counsel
Peck and Wolf Attorney at Law
105 West Adams Street
34th Floor
Chicago, Illinois 60603
(312) 263-5022

Representative Beryl Anthony (D., Arkansas)

Anthony, who was elected to the House in 1978, lost the 1992 Democratic primary to Bill McCuen after it was disclosed that he had 109 overdrafts at the House bank.

His wife, Sheila Foster Anthony, was appointed by President Clinton to be the Assistant secretary for legislative affairs at the Justice Department. She is the sister of former White House aide Vince Foster.

Anthony says when he left the House, he had offers from numerous law firms but signed on with the Washington office of Winston & Strawn, a Chicago-based firm, as a partner and its director of legislation and regulatory practice. "I had a hard time making a decision," he said. "I had some very good competing offers."

Anthony now represents the American Hospital Association on health care issues. A spokesman for the association told *National Journal* that Anthony was hired because of his "knowledge of the Clinton inner circle and his long friendship with Clinton." He also represents the Walt Disney Company.

While in the House, Anthony was the chairman of the Democratic Congressional Campaign Committee and a member of the Ways and Means Committee.

See also the chapter "The Revolving Door."

Business Address	*Home Address*
Winston & Strawn	3900 Macomb Street, N.W.
1400 L Street	Washington, D.C. 20016
Washington, D.C. 20005	(202) 686-6768
(202) 457-5671	

Senator William Armstrong (R., Colorado)

Armstrong was elected to the House in 1972 where he served until he was elected to the Senate in 1978. He returned home to Denver after his retirement from the Senate in 1990. "I'm back in business and spend about two-thirds of my time in business, mortgage banking, real estate and one-third in ministry," Armstrong told us. "I do a lot of evangelistic speaking."

"It's unlikely that I'd ever run again. It was a great experience. I was in Washington for 18 years, and we have a lot of close friends that we treasure, but I didn't find it hard to leave. In a certain sense, I never left Colorado. I didn't feel burned out in the slightest. I just felt like it was time to give someone else a chance. Never felt I got out of politics. I was involved last year in the Senate campaign in Colorado.

"Some people in public life are consumed by it. The last person we want in public office is a professional officeholder. The people we want in public office are people who see themselves in the mainstream of American life. If they don't they become somewhat a ruling elite. It's tragic for the country, and it's tragic for them. It's unfortunate when someone has to have a 'Senator' or 'Congressman' in front of their names."

Business Address
1625 Broadway, Suite 780
Denver, Colorado 80202
(303) 595-3828

Representative Les Aspin (D, Wisconsin)

Aspin was elected to the House in 1970, where he served until President Clinton named him Secretary of Defense in 1993. He resigned on December 15, 1993.

He is now the Arleigh A. Burke chair in Strategy at the Center for Strategic and International Studies in Washington.

Business Address
The Center for Strategic and International Studies
1800 K. Street, N.W.
Suite 400
Washington, D.C. 20006
(202) 775-3170

Representative Chester Atkins (D., Massachusetts)

Atkins was elected to the House in 1984. He lost the 1992 Democratic primary after it was disclosed that he had 127 overdrafts at the House bank.

After he left office, he worked with the Washington-based Wilderness Society for six months. Atkins has since returned home to Massachusetts, where he is a principal with ADS Ventures, which builds assisted-living centers.

Business Address
ADS Ventures
100 Main Street
Suite 230
Concord, Massachusetts 01742
(508) 369-1920

Representative Les AuCoin (D., Oregon)

AuCoin was elected to the House in 1974. In 1992, he gave up his House seat to mount an unsuccessful challenge against Senator Bob Packwood. He later joined the law firm of Bogle & Cates as the chairman of its government relations group; he is a lobbyist for American Forest and Paper Association, Confederated Tribes, Global Forestry Management Group, Harsch Financial Company, the International Paper Company, and the Northwest Forest Resource Council, among other clients.

Business Address
Bogle & Cates
1229 Pennsylvania Avenue, N.W., Suite 875
Washington, D.C. 20004
(202) 293-3600

Representative Robert Badham (R., California)

Badham was elected to the House in 1976 and retired in 1988. Now living in Newport Beach, California, Badham told us that he does some government relations consulting, trust, asset, and property management. Badham says that he gets back to Washington quite a bit but that he is mostly retired and is learning how to play golf. "Wild horses couldn't drag me back into politics," he said.

Badham converted approximately $40,000 in leftover campaign funds to his personal use.

Business Address
Robert E. Badham Associates
881 Dover Drive, Suite 14
Newport Beach, California 92260
(714) 645-6186

Home Address
1327 Antiqua Way
Newport Beach, California 92660
(714) 631-0211

Senator Howard Baker (R., Tennessee)

Baker was elected to the Senate in 1966 and retired in 1984 after serving as Senate Republican Leader from 1978 to 1984. He was President Reagan's chief of staff from 1987 to 1988. His father, Howard Baker, Sr., served in the House from 1951 to 1964. His father-in-law was Senator Everitt M. Dirksen of Illinois. And Baker's stepmother, Irene Bailey Baker, also served in the House when she was elected to finish his father's term following the senior Baker's death in 1964.

When Baker left the White House in 1988, he became a partner in the law firm of Baker, Worthington, Crossley, Stansberry & Woolf. The firm is registered to lobby for foreign and domestic clients, and has offices in Washington and Huntsville, Tennessee, where Baker has a home.

The firm's clients have included Argo Air, Airship International, Austrian Airlines, Bechtel Aviation Services, Burger King Corporation, Communications Counsel, Inc., Continental Airlines, Dallas/Fort Worth International Airport, Day & Zimmerman, DHL Worldwide Express, Duty Free International, Inc., EDS Corporation, Executive Air Fleets, Inc., Federal Express Corporation, Grand Metropolitan, Incorporated, Guiness Import Company, International Business Machines Corporation, Inturbine Corporation, Hashemite Kingdom of Jordan, Landauer Corporation, Los Angeles County Transportation Committee, Morrison Knudsen Corporation, Mutual Guaranty Corporation, National Business Aircraft, Nolisair (National Air Canada), North Carolina Air Cargo Authority, Occidental Petroleum Corporation, Pennzoil Company, Pillsbury Company, Pratt & Whitney, Ralston Purina/Brenmer Industries, Ryder Airline Services, Inc., Ryder System, Inc., Safe Flight Instrument Corporation, Schering Plough Corporation, Southern California Edison Corporation Company, Sprint Communications, U.S.T., Inc.; and United Technologies Corporation.

Business Address
Baker, Worthington, Crossley, Stansberry & Woolf
801 Pennsylvania Avenue, N.W., Suite 80
Washington, D.C. 20004
(202) 508-3400

Home Address
P.O. Box 8
Huntsville, Tennessee 37756
(615) 663-2321

Representative Doug Barnard (D., Georgia)

Barnard was elected to the House in 1976 and retired in 1992. He underwent quadruple bypass surgery in 1993 and said that he was "completely retiring." After his 1991 banking reform bill was killed in the House, Barnard told the *Atlanta Journal and Constitution* that "I was just so frustrated, exhausted, and absolutely discouraged with the whole process."

In 1993, Barnard converted $80,000 in leftover campaign funds to his personal use. The Associated Press reported in February 1994 that Barnard also intends to convert the remaining $172,473 to personal use: "I've made a decision and I'm paying about $70,000 in taxes . . . It's my business and I just don't care to talk about it."

Home Address
15 Indian Cove Road
Augusta, Georgia 30909
(706) 855-9049

Representative Michael Barnes (D., Maryland)

Barnes, who was elected to the House in 1978, gave up his seat to run for the Senate in 1986. He lost the Democratic primary to the eventual winner, Barbara Mikulski, and then joined the Washington law firm of Arent, Fox, Kinter, Plotkin & Kahn as a partner. In June 1993, Barnes left Arent, Fox to become a partner at another Washington law firm, Hogan & Hartson. His primary client was the exiled president of Haiti, Jean Bertrand-Aristide.

Still active in the Democratic National Committee, Barnes chaired the party's 1992 effort in Maryland and serves on a variety of local and national political organizations. He is also the chairman of the Washington-based Center for National Policy.

See chapter "The Revolving Door."

Business Address
Hogan & Hartson
555 13th Street, N.W.
Washington, D.C. 20004
(202) 637-5695

Home Address
3948 Baltimore Street
Kensington, Maryland 20895
(301) 933-7474

Representative Steve Bartlett (R., Texas)

Bartlett was elected to the House in 1982 and served until 1991, when he gave up his seat to wage a successful campaign to become mayor of Dallas. Before being sworn is as mayor, Bartlett told the *Bond Buyer* that his four years in Congress left him certain that cities must solve their own problems and should expect little help from Congress. "Cities that are successful rely on their own abilities and their own citizens," he said. "I can't think of many issues on which Congress is the solution. I can think of a fair number where they are the problem."

Business Address
Mayor's Office
1500 Marilla-5EN
Dallas, Texas 75201
(214) 670-4054

Representative Jim Bates (D., California)

Bates was elected to the House in 1982 and served until Republican Randy "Duke" Cunningham defeated him by 1,600 votes in 1990. Bates's political career ran into trouble when the Standards of Official Conduct Committee reproved him in 1989 after a female aide accused him of sexual harassment. In 1992, he made an ill-fated bid to recaputure his congressional seat; he lost in the Democratic primary.

After his 1990 loss, Bates stayed in Washington and worked at a variety of things, even selling insurance. In 1994, he returned to his old San Diego district and has begun working as a campaign consultant with his former adviser, Larry Remer. He is also working as a business consultant with former California Representative Mervyn Dymally.

"Three years have gone by, which is a long time," Bates told the *San Diego Union-Tribune* in March 1994. "Two things happened in that time. One, it doesn't hurt anymore, and it used to hurt like someone cut my back open every time I even thought about it. And two, I'm starting to enjoy my life again, just living every day. The main fault I have is that I'm still a little bitter. And I suppose I ought to get over that."

Bates decided against becoming a lobbyist because "I didn't want to go back to the Hill in a lesser position and run into people I'd been with, who knew me when, and get into all that again."

Leaving office after a loss, and with the taint of a scandal was tough for Bates. "People don't give a [expletive] anymore," he told the *Union Tribune*. "It's funny how people -- in your own family, even -- treat you differently when you've lost, people who are closest to you. I guess that's to be expected. I guess everyone reads more into the position than you think. You think at the time it's really you. But it's not. It's the position."

Business Address
3609 Fourth Avenue
San Diego, California 92103
(619) 295-6923

Representative Berkley Bedell (D., Iowa)

Elected to the House in 1974, Bedell retired in 1986. Although he says that he has retired as far as having a paying job, Bedell remains active in two political areas: alternative health care and medicine, and alternative energy.

Bedell was appointed to an advisory commission on alternative medical practices for the National Institutes of Health. "I'm very happy with what I'm doing, it is very exciting," Bedell said. "I was one of the old members, retirement has been no problem at all for me."

Washington Address
435 New Jersey Avenue, S.E.
Washington, D.C. 20003
(202) 543-3257

Home Address
15712 Rusty Road
Spirit Lake, Iowa 51360
(712) 336-5070
Winter Home Address
1807 Snook Drive
Naples, Florida 33962

Representative Charles Bennett (D., Florida)

Bennett was elected to the House in 1948 and served until his retirement in 1992. Today, the 84-year-old Bennett is a professor of government at Jacksonville University. Bennett, who for many years was a powerful member of the House Armed Services Committee, was also a visiting professor at the University of Florida, the University of North Florida, Edwards Waters College, and the

Bennett told us that he and his wife spend January to July in Florida and the rest of the year in Falls Church, Virginia. After he left office, Bennett donated $270,835 in leftover campaign funds to the National Park Service.

Business Address
Jacksonville University
Jacksonville, Florida 32211

Home Address
1611 Riverside Avenue
Jacksonville, Florida 32204
(904) 354-7689

Senator Lloyd Bentsen (D., Texas)

Bentsen was elected to the House in 1948 and served for six years before he quit to build a successful business career in Texas. He was elected to the Senate in 1970 when he defeated the Republican nominee, George Bush. In the Senate, Bentsen was known as a master politician. He won rave reviews as Michael Dukakis's running mate in 1988 and in December 1992, President-Elect Bill Clinton named him Treasury Secretary.

Bentsen is relishing his role in the Cabinet. "This is an exciting time to be a Treasury Secretary," he said. "I like to tell the staff that in our history, there have been times when the spotlight was on the military or the diplomats at the State Department. Today, the focus is on the economy -- and Treasury is playing the leading role."

Business Address
Secretary of the Treasury
Room 3330
Treasury Department
15th & Pennsylvania Avenue, N.W.
Washington, D.C. 20220
(202) 622-1100

Representative Ed Bethune (R., Arkansas)

Elected to the House in 1978, Bethune served three terms before he gave up his seat to make an unsuccessful bid against Democrat David Pryor for the Senate in 1984.

Bethune now works for his former law firm in his old hometown of Searcy, Arkansas. He returned briefly to Washington during the Bush Administration when his wife served as social secretary to Vice President Dan Quayle and his wife, Marilyn. Bethune practiced law in Washington during this period, but when the Bush Administration ended in 1993, the Bethunes tried another kind of adventure. They set out on their boat for a trans-Atlantic trip. After just six days at sea, however, they lost their vessel during a storm. "So we came back to Arkansas," Bethune said.

Today his work as the general counsel for the 7,000-member FBI Agents Association comprises about 30 percent of his law practice.

Business Address
Bethune Law Firm
P.O. Box 200
Searcy, Arkansas 72143
(501) 268-3055

Representative Mario Biaggi (D., New York)

Biaggi was elected to the House in 1968 as one of the most decorated police officers in New York City's history. He resigned on August 5, 1988, after he was convicted of bribery, racketeering, conspiracy, and extortion in the Wedtech Corporation scandal and sentenced to eight years in prison. In 1988, Biaggi ran for reelection but lost to challenger Eliot Engel. In May 1992, he was released from federal prison, because of ill health, after serving 22 months, and he subsequently challenged Engel in the 1992 Democratic primary. He lost the race, 76 percent to 24 percent.

Today, Biaggi is living in his old district in the Bronx and working on his memoirs. He had some advice for indicted Representative Dan Rostenkowski in *Newsday* in June 1994. "Have faith and you'll endure. This is a blip in the universe of Rosty's life. He will go through purgatory for a while. If he doesn't have the strength, he's in for a sorrowful, sorrowful life."

Biaggi used $386,064 in campaign funds to pay for legal fees resulting from his criminal trial.

Business Address	*Home Address*
299 Broadway	3333 Henry Hudson Parkway
New York, N.Y. 10007	Bronx, New York 10463
(212) 233-8000	(212) 549-1283

Representative Lindy Boggs (D., Louisiana)

Boggs was elected to the House on March 29, 1973 to fill the seat left vacant by the death of her husband, House Majority Leader Hale Boggs. She retired in 1990 at age 74.

See also the chapter "Going Home Again: Lindy Boggs."

Business Address
Advisor to the President
Tulane University
New Orleans, Louisiana 70118
(504) 581-1441

Representative Edward Boland (D., Massachusetts)

Elected to the House the same year as his good friend and longtime Washington roommate, Tip O'Neill. Boland retired in 1988. He authored the now famous Boland Amendment which banned the United States from directly or indirectly aiding the Nicaraguan contras. Former White House aide Lieutenant Colonel

Oliver North, among others, was accused of violating the Boland Amendment during the Iran-contra scandal. "They clearly violated the law," Boland said in 1988. "And they got caught."

At age 83, Boland lives with his family in his former district. During his 36 years in the House, Boland was a rarity by having just twice mailed out newsletters to his constituents, and his one and only press conference was to announced his retirement.

"I'm not sure somebody ought to stay here for 36 years, I'm not sure of that," Boland told the *Boston Globe* in October 1988. "If I had the choice to do it over again, would I do it over again? No, I don't think so. I think one of the reasons for that is you go through the same thing every year . . . you're chairing that committee, you have the same problems, you have different personalities . . . after awhile it gets to be a bit boring, and for the chairman of a subcommittee, he does a lot of work, he has to be there . . . a lot of members don't join in."

In his autobiography, *Man of the House*, O'Neill described the living situation the two young Massachusetts congressmen had. "Eddie was a bachelor, and he brought down all the home furnishings he owned -- a toaster and a coffee pot." O'Neill wrote. "He'd always do the laundry and keep the place clean . . . we never cooked a meal there . . . the only four items ever seen in that fridge were orange juice, diet soda, beer, and cigars."

"I had a busy life," Boland told the *Boston Globe*. I should have written it all down like Tip did and had a book. I'd have become a millionaire."

Home Address
87 Ridgeway Circle
Springfield, Massachusetts 01118
(413) 734-1739

Representative William Boner (D., Tennessee)

Boner was elected to the House in 1978 and served until he resigned on October 5, 1987 to become the mayor of Nashville, Tennessee. In 1985, the *Nashville Tennessean* published a series of articles alleging that Boner had violated financial disclosure laws, misused campaign funds, and accepted illegal gifts. The Justice Department investigated charges that Boner had accepted nearly $50,000 in bribes from a Nashville defense contractor, but took no action against Boner. The House Standards of Official Conduct Committee also investigated allegations against Boner but he was elected mayor before the committee acted.

After his term as mayor term was over in 1991, Boner moved to Thompkinsville, Kentucky, and ran a business. Today, he has moved back home to Nashville and says that he has changed his life. "There was a period I was so wrapped up in my work that it clouded my judgment," Boner told the Associated Press in July 1994. "I wasn't a very good Christian witness."

Boner now does public relations for gospel singer Bobby Jones and devotes himself to his church. "The hardest thing to do is to admit you've made mistakes," he said. "I've learned it's not so bad for a man to cry. The Bible is the best self-help course there is, the greatest teacher in life."

Boner used $197,005 in campaign funds to pay legal fees resulting from the Justice Department and Ethics Committee investigations.

Home Telephone
(615) 370-1669

Representative Don Bonker (D., Washington)

Bonker, who was elected to the House in 1974, gave up his seat to run for the Senate in 1988. He lost the Democratic primary to Mike Lowry.

Bonker became the executive vice president of APCO Associates, a Washington-based lobbying firm. His clients have included the American Maritime Congress, Heart of America Northwest, Minnesota World Trade Center Corporation, and State Farm Insurance Company. He is also the president and Chief Executive Officer of International Management and Development Institute.

Business Address
APCO Associates
1155 21st Street, N.W.
Suite 1000
Washington, D.C. 20036
(202) 778-1019

Representative Douglas Bosco (D., California)

Bosco was elected to the House in 1982. He lost the 1990 election to Republican Frank Riggs. In 1994, Bosco challenged Representative Dan Hamburg -- who beat Riggs in the 1992 general election -- in the Democratic primary. Hamburg won the primary after he attacked Bosco as a lobbyist for Pacific Lumber and his endorsement by the district's logging companies.

"Everyone in the 1st District loves redwood trees," Bosco told the *Los Angeles Times*. "It's just that half the people love them horizontal. Dan [Hamburg] can go to tears over a marbled murrelit. I'm more concerned about the kid whose world falls apart because Dad got laid off."

Since mid-1993, as an attorney, Bosco was paid approximately $15,000 a month by Headwaters Forest Pacific Lumber Company to lobby against Hamburg's proposal to ban logging in the Headwaters Forest and to limit cutting in a surrounding 69-square-mile buffer zone.

"For years I was one of the party stalwarts, the guy who threw the fund-raisers, who poured thousands into other Democrats' campaigns," Bosco told the *Los Angeles Times*. "Now I'm kind of like the guest crashing the banquet, spoiling the party. It's strange, but in one sense, it's sort of liberating."

In a bizarre race that pitted two former congressmen against an incumbent, Hamburg lost to the man he had defeated for the House seat, Frank Riggs, in the 1994 general election.

Home Telephone
(707) 874-1119

Senator Rudy Boschwitz (R., Minnesota)

Boschwitz was elected to the Senate in 1978 and served two terms until he lost in 1990 to Democrat Paul Wellstone. He returned home to Minnesota as the Chief Executive Officer of his large lumber and hardware chain, Home Value.

Boschwitz recently said that he wants a rematch against Wellstone in 1996.

In early 1994, Boschwitz was sued by Jon Grunseth, a 1990 candidate for governor in Minnesota. Grunseth alleged that Boschwitz had promised to pay off his $100,000 campaign debt if Grunseth withdrew from the race after several allegations of sexual misconduct were made public. Grunseth left the race in late October of 1990. The case has been dismissed.

"I've never been sued before, and it wasn't one of the more pleasurable experiences of my life," Boschwitz told the *Minneapolis Star Tribune*.

Business Address
Home Value
5401 East River Road
Minneapolis, Minnesota 55421
(612) 571-2636

Representative Beau Boulter (R., Texas)

Boulter defeated Democratic incumbent Jack Hightower in 1984 to win a House seat. He gave up his seat to make an unsuccessful bid for the Senate in 1988.

In 1994, Boulter was named a fellow at Harvard University's John F. Kennedy School of Government.

Business Address
John F. Kennedy School of Government
Harvard University
79 John F. Kennedy Street
Cambridge, Massachusetts 02138

Senator Barbara Boxer (D., California)

Boxer was elected to the House in 1982. She was elected to the Senate,where she currently serves, in 1992.

Business Address
843 Dirksen Senate
 Office Building
Washington, D.C. 20510
(202) 224-5017

Representative Joseph Brennan (D., Maine)

Brennan served as the governor of Maine for eight years before he was elected to the House in 1986. He gave up his House seat to challenge Republican Governor John McKernan in 1990 but lost in a close race. Brennan once again ran for the governorship in 1994, but was defeated by Independent candidate Angus King.

Business Address
P.O. Box 147
Portland, Maine 04112
(207) 878-1994

Representative Robin Britt (D., North Carolina)

Britt was elected to the House in 1982 but lost his bid for reelection in 1984. In 1993, Britt was named North Carolina's Secretary of Human Resources by Governor James D. Hunt, Jr.

Business Address	*Home Address*
North Carolina Human Resources	600 North Elam Avenue
P.O. Box 29530	Greensboro, North Carolina 27408
Raleigh, North Carolina 27626	(919) 288-8544
(919) 733-4534	

Representative William Broomfield (R., Michigan)

Broomfield was elected to the House in 1956 and served until he retired in 1992. He converted $517,688 in leftover campaign funds to his private charitable trust in 1993. He also transferred $303,000 in leftover campaign funds to his political action committee.

Broomfield is retired and lives in the Washington suburb of Kensington, Maryland.

Home Address
9910 East Bexhill Drive
Kensington, Maryland 20895
(301) 942-4882

Senator Hank Brown (R., Colorado)

Brown was elected to the House in 1980 and to the Senate, where he currently serves, in 1990.

Business Address
716 Hart Senate Office Building
Washington, D.C. 20510
(202) 224-5941

Senator James Broyhill (R., North Carolina)

Broyhill was elected to the House in 1962, where he served until he was appointed to the Senate on July 14, 1986, to fill the seat left vacant by the death of Senator John East. He lost the 1986 general election to Democrat Terry Sanford.

Broyhill then returned to North Carolina, where he worked in the administration of Republican Governor James Martin as the chairman of the North Carolina Economic Development Board. From 1989 to 1991, he served as the Secretary of the North Carolina Department of Commerce.

Today, Broyhill serves on a number of university boards in North Carolina and remains active in statewide bond issues. He says that he and his wife, Louise, live in Winston-Salem in the same neighborhood as two of their three children.

Home Address
1930 Virginia Road
Winston-Salem, North Carolina 27104
(910) 727-1396

Representative Terry Bruce (D., Illinois)

Bruce was elected to the House in 1984, but lost the 1992 Democratic primary to Glenn Poshard. Bruce, who'd been a member of the powerful Energy and Commerce Committee, landed a lobbying job as the vice president of federal relations for Ameritech (American Information Technologies Corporation).

Business Address
Ameritech
1401 H Street, N.W.
Suite 1020
Washington, D.C. 20005
(202) 326-3800

Representative Jack Buechner (R., Missouri)

Buechner, who was elected to the House in 1986, lost in 1990 to Democrat Joan Kelly Horn by 54 votes after a highly negative campaign.

Buechner recently wrote about his experiences in the House:

"November 3, 1984, 8:10 CST: I felt the excitement of seeing Leslie Stahl project me the winner in what she called the 'Beginning of a Reagan landslide!' Unfortunately, Leslie was two years premature. That 1 percent loss encouraged me to try again. In 1986, I became the only Republican in the country to unseat an incumbent for federal office.

"Sixty-five days later, I raised my hand for the oath that brought me into the 100th Congress. To many observers it was a watershed Congress, not for its monumental legislation but as the last time the words collegiality and incumbency had much meaning.

"Candidates for Congress, incumbents and challengers alike, had for years been 'running against Congress.' Sooner or later the constituents were bound to start figuring that if it was such a bad place, then maybe their Congressman might not be so great either. Sooner became the present.

"But as the nation, especially the Washington Establishment, celebrated 200 years of democratic representative government it was a truly magnificent time to be a member of Congress. Most fostered no illusion that they were a Jefferson, Clay or Webster . . . or, for that matter, a Goldwater or Fenwick. Still, the history and the future of that great chamber raised you, and your peers, to a special level of appreciation of who you were. It was a special time to be in a special place. Never will I have a similar experience. Combined with being one of the first freshmen ever appointed to the Budget Committee and a plum assignment on Science and Technology, the headlines could have made me aloof. Twelve years in public life acted as a reality check.

"A smashing 2-1 victory in 1988 helped my advance into the Republican leadership as deputy whip. Legislation on space and biotechnology that I authored was enacted. It should have been heaven.

"Sadly, corruption allegations against the Speaker of the House began to solidify. The partisanship that surfaced was more virulent than anything before the 'Pax Bicentennium.' Jim Wright's peccadilloes, the House bank, and the pay raise fed the anti-incumbency movement . . . next came term limits . . . talk show frenzies . . . Prime Time . . . Hard Copy . . . 60 Minutes. 'Congressman' became an epithet, not a title.

"Fundraising, while trying to perform campaign practices, seemed ludicrous. Much of the joy and satisfaction of public service began to ebb. Weekend trips to the district seemed longer and longer. My divorce became final while McDonnell-Douglas and Chrysler laid off 20,000 workers in my district.

"Everything I was working on seemed impossible or without redemption, including the compromise on the budget that I felt could end the Bush presidency. The President asked me to support him. I did knowing it was an anathema to my base of conservative support.

"November 3, 1990 (the anniversary of my only other loss in 16 years of politics): The last precinct puts me down by 50 votes in a campaign during which I was portrayed as a pig at a trough.

"At night, when Congress is in session, if I see the light in the dome I ache for the halcyon time, no matter how few. But when I walk into my home, see my wife, Nancy, and our infant son, Charlie, I question if it is worth the price to serve in today's Congress. I am proud to have served but happy that I am no longer there."

Today, Buechner lives in McLean, Virginia, with his wife and small children. "I go back about once a month to Republican membership groups," he said. "The thing that has struck me is that the complaints about the system haven't changed, but the relationship between the members and constituents has gotten worse. A serious problem is the attitude of the people, a sense of helplessness. I think it is just the overall attitude in office. A guy like Ross Perot fans that flame.

"I've had people say, 'Come on back and do it,' but I've paid my dues and I've done my public service -- which I believe that it is. I would be lying to you if I said I didn't miss some of it, the comradire."

Buechner, as senior partner in the Hawthorn Group, is lobbying as a registered foreign agent for Albania.

Business Address	*Home Address*
The Hawthorn Group, L.C.	8956 Old Tolson Mill Road
1300 North 17th Street	McLean, Virginia 22102
Suite 1330	(703) 893-5107
Arlington, Virginia 22209	
(703) 312-5326	

Representative Sala Burton (D., California)

Sala Burton took over the House seat left vacant by the death of her husband, Phil Burton, on June 28, 1983. She died in office on February 1, 1987.

Senator Quentin Burdick (D., North Dakota)

Burdick was elected to the House in 1958 and to the Senate in 1960. He died in office on September 8, 1992.

Representative Albert Bustamante (D., Texas)

Bustamante, who was elected to the House in 1984, was defeated in the 1992 election by Republican Henry Bonilla. He pleaded not guilty in March 1993 to federal racketeering, conspiracy, and bribery charges. In October 1993, he was sentenced to three and a half years in prison and was ordered to pay $55,100 in fines and court costs. He is currently free on bond pending appeal.

Business Address
c/o Herndon, Brown & Campion
222 Main Plaza
San Antonio, Texas 78205
(210) 227-5161

Representative Beverly Byron (D., Maryland)

Byron, who was elected to the House in 1978, was defeated in the 1992 Democratic primary. She now serves on the Commission on Defense Base Closing and Realignment.

Home Address
306 Grove Boulevard
Frederick, Maryland 21701
(301) 663-5626

Representative Ben Nighthorse Campbell (D., Colorado)

Campbell was elected to the House in 1986 and to the Senate, where he currently serves, in 1992.

Business Address
380 Russell Senate Office Building
Washington, D.C. 20510
(202) 224-5852

Representative Carroll Campbell (R., South Carolina)

Campbell was elected to the House in 1978, where he served until he was elected governor of South Carolina in 1986. Mentioned as a possible 1996 presidential candidate, Campbell recently took himself out of the running and became president of the American Council of Life Insurance when his term was over in 1995. Another former lawmaker, Dan Mica, is the council's executive vice president.

"My heart told me to run, but my head said to look after the family first," Campbell said, adding that he was not wealthy enough to run for President. The council's president, Richard Schweiker, a former Republican Senator from Pennsylvania, reportedly earned more than $700,000 in salary and benefits in 1993.

Business Address
Governor
The State of South Carolina
P.O. Box 11369
Columbia, South Carolina 29211
(803) 734-9818

American Council of Life Insurance
1001 Pennsylvania Avenue, N.W.
Washington, D.C. 20004
(202) 624-2121

Representative Tom Campbell (R., California)

Campbell, who was elected to the House in 1988, gave up his seat to run for the Senate in 1992, but lost the Republican primary.

Campbell was the founder of the Republican Majority Coalition, an organization designed to counteract the influence of the Christian Right on the Republican Party. "We are a nation based on respect for people who believe in different ways about God and religion and faith," Campbell told the *San Diego Union-Tribune*. "It goes against that tendency of tolerance to say, 'If you are unwilling to [recognize] Christian values as predominant . . . then you have no place in government.'"

Campbell, who once edited the *Harvard Law Review*, became a professor at the Stanford University Law School after his term was over. Then, in 1993, he won a special election to the California State Senate.

"If I ever run for United States Senate again and if I win, I will be a much better United States Senator for having been a state senator," Campbell told the *Sacramento Bee* in April 1994. "I could have run for lieutenant governor . . . I chose this, and I am delighted with this choice. There is so much substance to this job as compared with those others. In contrast, in Washington the committees were not obliged even to hear bills that I drafted.

"I am not engaged in an effort to advance myself or make a publicity splash. I am interested in building a solid record of accomplishment . . . That, I think is the best way to pursue public office."

Business Address
State Capitol
Sacramento, California 95814
(415) 725-2098
and Stanford University Law School
Crown Law Quad
Stanford, California 94305
(415) 725-2098

Representative William Carney (R., New York)

Carney, who was elected to the House in 1978, retired in 1986 when polls showed that he would not win reelection because of his support for the Shoreham nuclear power plant. After he left the House, Carney remained in Washington and set up a lobbying practice with his congressional office manager, Jill Sirianni.

Carney converted $83,695 in leftover campaign funds to personal use.

Business Address	*Home Address*
523 Seventh Street, S.E.	523 Seventh Street, S.E.
Washington, D.C. 20003	Washington, D.C. 20003
(202) 543-5237	(202) 544-8195

Representative Thomas Carper (D., Delaware)

Carper, who was elected to the House in 1982, was elected governor of Delaware in 1992.

Business Address	*Home Address*
State of Delaware	Woodburn
P.O. Box 1401	151 Kings Highway
Dover, Delaware 19901	Dover, Delaware 19901
(302) 739-4101	(302) 739-5656

Representative Rod Chandler (R., Washington)

Chandler, who was elected to the House in 1982, lost his bid for the Senate in 1992 to Democrat Patty Murray. Chandler is now a senior associate with the Washington lobbying firm of Downey Chandler, Inc., along with former Representative Tom Downey (D., N.Y.).

Commenting on the state of Congress today, Chandler told *Time* magazine in June 1994, that ethics have taken hold in the House: "It was a common practice in those days [the 1950s and '60s] for a lobbyist to come to a member of Congress and hand him an envelope and say, 'Here, this is for your campaign.' It was a nod-and-a-wink thing. 'If you use it on your campaign, fine. If not, that's up to you.' Nothing even approaching that happens anymore."

Chandler has $61,661 remaining in his campaign account.

Business Address
Downey Chandler, Inc.
1401 I. Street, N.W.
Suite 1210
Washington, D.C. 20005
(202) 898-6458

Representative Eugene Chappie (R., California)

Elected to the House in 1980, Chappie retired in 1986 and joined the Washington lobbying firm of Fleishman-Hillard, Inc. after leaving. He used leftover campaign funds to make $41,000 in contributions to scholarships.

Chappie died on May 31, 1992.

Representative Bill Chappell (D., Florida)

Elected to the House in 1968, Chappell was defeated in 1988 by Republican Craig James after being named in the 'Ill Wind' Pentagon procurement scandal. He died of bone cancer on March 30, 1989.

Chappell converted $34,000 in leftover campaign funds to personal use before his death and his estate received an additional $2,324.

Representative Dick Cheney (R., Wyoming)

Cheney was elected to the House in 1978, having returned to his home state of Wyoming to run for Congress after serving as President Gerald Ford's Chief of Staff. He left the House in 1989, when President Bush named him Secretary of

Defense. Following the Bush Administration, he again moved home to Wyoming and is considering a race for the presidency in 1996.

Cheney has $73,849 remaining in his congressional campaign account.

See chapter "A Place in History: Dick Cheney"

Business Address
American Enterprise Institute for Public Policy Research
1150 17th Street, N.W. Suite 1100
Washington, D.C. 20036
(202) 862-5800

Senator Lawton Chiles (D., Florida)

Elected to the Senate in 1970 as the energetic "Walkin' Lawton", Chiles retired in 1988, saying: "I wasn't looking forward to another six years in the Senate. What that inner voice told me was, it was time to serve out the 18 years and move over to let someone with the enthusiasm and zeal take over. At some stage, maybe there is a burnout."

Chiles overcame his burnout to run for governor of Florida in 1990 and win. He won a tough reelection bid in 1994 against Republican candidate Jeb Bush.

Business Address
Office of the Governor
The Capitol
Tallahassee, Florida 32399
(904) 488-4441

Representative James McClure Clarke (D., North Carolina)

Clarke was elected to the House in 1982, but lost the 1984 election to Republican Bill Hendon. In 1986, he came back and beat Hendon for the seat, but lost in 1990 to Republican Charles Taylor. Today, he is a part-time farmer outside his old hometown of Asheville, North Carolina. "We have a farm," Clarke said. "Principally, apples and a small raspberry crop. A pretty good apple crop. There's always something to do on a farm."

Clarke is still active in community affairs and is a director of the Community Foundation in Asheville and the North Carolina Environmental Defense Fund.

Home Address
15 Clarke Lane
Fairview, North Carolina 28730
(704) 628-2616

Representative Bill Cobey (R., North Carolina)

Cobey, who was elected to the House in 1984, served only one term before he was defeated in 1986. Before his election, Cobey was the athletic director of the University of North Carolina. After his defeat, Governor James Martin appointed him Deputy Secretary of Transportation and then, in 1989, Secretary of the Department of Environment, Health and Natural Resources. Today, Cobey works as town manager of Morrisville, North Carolina. "I thoroughly enjoyed working in state government," Cobey said. "Best years professionally. North Carolina has never had a more able and honorable governor [than Martin]."

Home Address
2410 Falls Drive
Chapel Hill, North Carolina 27514
(919) 383-7032

Representative Tony Coelho (D., California)

Elected to the House in 1978, Coelho was on the congressional fast track and had risen to House Majority Whip when he abruptly resigned in June 1989, after an investigation was launched into alleged campaign payoffs by savings-and-loan executives. He has maintained his Washington contacts and was a prominent adviser to senior members of the Clinton Administration.

In August 1994, President Clinton named Coelho special adviser to the Democratic National Committee, where he became the party's chief spokesman and campaign guru. In accepting the position, he announced that the DNC job was temporary and that he would return to his Wall Street investment firm after the November 1994 elections. Coelho has worked on Wall Street since he left Congress in 1989 and has become a millionaire with Wertheim Schroder. His wife, Phyllis, told *The Washington Post*, "Life is better now, definitely, definitely, definitely."

Coelho converted approximately $57,000 in campaign funds to personal use after he left office, including $30,000 to pay for legal bills relating to investigations by the House Standards of Official Conduct Committee and the Justice Department.

Business Address
President and CEO
Wertheim Schroder Investment Services, Inc.
Equitable Center
787 Seventh Avenue
New York, N.Y. 10019-6016
(212) 492-6423

Representative E. Thomas Coleman (R., Missouri)

Elected to the House in 1976, Coleman was unseated in 1992 by Democrat Pat Danner. After a short stint as a consultant to the Student Loan Marketing Association (Sallie Mae), Coleman joined the Washington law firm of Clohan & Dean.

Business Address
Clohan & Dean
1101 Vermont Avenue, N.W.
Suite 400
Washington, D.C. 20005
(202) 289-3900

Representative Silvio Conte (R., Massachusetts)

Conte was elected to the House in 1958 and served until he died in office in February 1991.

Campaign funds amounting to $67,159 paid for Conte's funeral, including a $40,000 tombstone.

Representative Barber Conable (R., New York)

Elected to the House in 1964, Conable retired in 1984. He now lives in Alexander, New York (population 400). "I wanted to come home where the roots were," he said. "My wife has been very supportive and I'm grateful. They live in an old farmhouse, where Conable says that he has planted 140 varieties of trees. "I'm a tree hugger. When I'm not running around trying to prove that I'm still relevant, I'm up there communing with nature." They have three daughters living near them in New York and a son living in Sarasota, Florida, whom Conable says they visit regularly.

As the ranking Republican on the House Ways and Means Committee, Conable was able to make a successful transition from public to private life. He was named to the boards of directors of several multinational corporations, including Pfizer Corporation and Corning Corporation, and to the board of the New York Stock Exchange. In 1986, he was named to be the president of the World Bank, which is headquartered in Washington. "There are lots of opportunities if you are willing to take them," Conable said. "I'm hooked on the issues of development and have done many things since then relating to development."

Conable is still active in Washington circles: He is the chairman of the executive committee of the board of regents of the Smithsonian Institution and is a trustee of the National Museum of the American Indian. "I'm an amateur anthropologist -- have been for years," Conable said.

Home Address
P.O. Box 218
Alexander, New York 14005
(716) 591-1233

Representative Tom Corcoran (R., Illinois)

Corcoran, who was elected to the House in 1976, gave up his seat to mount an unsuccessful challenge to Senator Charles Percy in the 1984 Republican primary. He lives in Chicago.

Representative Lawrence Coughlin (R., Pennsylvania)

Elected to the House in 1968, Coughlin retired in 1992 and joined the Washington office of Eckert, Seamans, Cherin & Mellott as senior counsel.

Coughlin's campaign committee closed, transferring $49,271 of leftover campaign funds to the Leadership Council PAC. He transferred $208,000 to the Coughlin Family Charitable Trust and made $65,156 in other political contributions.

Business Address
Eckert, Seamans, Cherin & Mellott
2100 Pennsylvania Avenue, N.W.
Suite #60
Washington, D.C. 20037
(202) 659-6600

Home Address
222 South Carolina Avenue, S.E.
Washington, D.C. 20003

Representative Jim Courter (R., New Jersey)

Elected to the House in 1978, Courter gave up his seat in 1989 to run for governor of New Jersey. After he lost to Democrat James Florio, Courter returned to the law practice he said he started 20 years ago. "I should have retired sooner," Courter said.

Courter, who'd been a member of the House Armed Services Committee, was hired by Grumman Corporation as a $3,000-a-month lobbyist. He dropped that contract in 1991 when President Bush appointed him to be the chairman of the Defense Base Closure Commission. He served until June 1994, when he resigned. In accepting his resignation, President Clinton praised Courter and said that his leadership "recommended base closures and realignments which will enable the federal government to save billions of dollars over the next several years."

Business Address
Courter, Kobert, et al.
1001 Route 517
Hackettstown, New Jersey 07840
(908) 852-2600

Representative John Cox (D., Illinois)

Elected to the House in 1990, Cox was unseated in 1992 by Republican Donald Manzullo. He has returned to Galena, Illinois, where he practices law.

Business Address
Cox Law Offices
612 Spring Street
P.O. Box 252
Galena, Illinois 61036
(815) 777-8180

Home Address
906 Third Street
Galena, Illinois 61036

Representative Larry Craig (R., Idaho)

Craig was elected to the House in 1980 and to the Senate, where he currently serves, in 1990.

Business Address
313 Hart Senate Office Building
Washington, D.C. 20510
(202) 224-2752

Senator Alan Cranston (D., California)

Elected to the Senate in 1968, Cranston retired in 1992. In 1991, the Senate Ethics Committee issued Cranston a 'harsh rebuke' for his actions on behalf of savings-and-loan executive owner Charles Keating, whose bankrupt S & L cost taxpayers an estimated $2 billion.

Cranston now lives in California and serves as the chairman of the California-based Gorbachev Foundation, U.S.A. and as the president of the U.S.-KYRGYZ Business Council in Washington.

Business Address
Gorbachev Foundation, USA
Box 29434
The Presidio
San Francisco. California 94129
(415) 771-4567

Home Address
27060 Old Trace Lane
Los Altos Hills, California 94022
(415) 948-6556

Representative Daniel Crane (R., Illinois)

Crane was elected to the House in 1978 but defeated in 1984 after he admitted having had a sexual relationship with a congressional page. Crane returned to his dental practice in Illinois; his brother, Phil, still serves in the House.

Business Address
3570 North Vermilion
Danville, Illinois 61832
(217) 442-5306

Representative George Crockett (D., Michigan)

Elected to the House in 1980, Crockett chose to retire in 1990 after surviving a tough primary challenge from Barbara-Rose Collins in 1988. He is retired and living in Washington.

Home Address
1630 Upshur Street, N.W.
Washington, D.C. 20011
(202) 726-7852

Representative Norman D'Amours (D., New Hampshire)

Elected to the House in 1974, D'Amours gave up his seat to unsuccessfully challenge Republican Senator Gordon Humphrey in 1984.

After he left the House, D'Amours joined former conservative Republican Representative John Rousselot of California in the Washington lobbying firm of Alcade, Rousselot & Fay. The firm represented the American Council of State Savings Supervisors, Bank of America NA & SA, Credit Union National Association, and Eli Lilly and Company.

In 1993, President Clinton appointed D'Amours as the chairman of the National Credit Union Association.

D'Amours used approximately $20,000 in leftover campaign funds from his Senate race to pay for personal items, including the purchase of a car.

Business Address
National Credit Union Administration
1775 Duke Street
Alexandria, Virginia 22314
(703) 518-6300

Home Address
8202 Lee Oaks Place, #303
Falls Church, Virginia 22046

Representative W.C. "Dan" Daniel (D., Virginia)

Elected to the House in 1968, Daniel died in office in January 1988, just four days after he announced his plans to retire. His estate received $112,910 in leftover campaign funds.

Representative William Dannemeyer (R., California)

Dannemeyer, who was elected to the House in 1978, gave up his seat to run for the Senate in 1992, but lost in the Republican primary. In 1994, he again ran for the Senate but lost the Republican primary to Representative Michael Huffington.

Business Address
1105 East Commonwealth
Fullerton, California 52631

Representative Hal Daub (R., Nebraska)

Elected to the House in 1980, Daub gave up his seat to challenge Senator David Karnes in the 1988 Republican primary. Karnes won the primary, and Daub waited two years and again ran for the Senate. He lost the 1990 race to Democratic Senator James Exon.

Daub has remained in Washington, working as a principal and director of federal government affairs for the accounting firm of Deloitte & Touche. He also maintains a home in Nebraska. His wife, Cindy, is the former chairwoman of the Copyright Royalty Tribunal, which President Clinton dissolved in late 1993. In 1988, she was the chairwoman of the Coalition of Asian-Americans for Bush/Quayle.

Business Address
Deloitte & Touche
1001 Pennsylvania Avenue, N.W.
Suite 350N
Washington, D.C. 20004
(202) 879-5375

Home Address
1204 South 99th Street
Omaha, Nebraska 68124

Representative Jack Davis (R., Illinois)

Elected to the House in 1986, Davis served one term before he was defeated in 1988 by Democrat George Sangmeister. Following his defeat, Davis returned to Illinois briefly. In late 1989, he was appointed assistant secretary for aviation matters at the Illinois Department of Transportation. Secretary of Defense Dick

Cheney named Davis a Deputy Assistant Secretary of the Air Force for readiness support in April 1990. Davis told *Roll Call* in 1990 that "about 200 members [of Congress] wrote letters on my behalf."

Davis has returned to Illinois.

Business Address
Frederic, Nessler & Associates
800 Myers Building
Springfield, Illinois 62701
(217) 753-5533

Representative Robert Davis (R., Michigan)

Elected to the House in 1978, Davis retired from office in 1992 rather than face voters after it was disclosed that he had 878 overdrafts at the House bank, the third highest total in the House. Davis also got into political hot water when it was disclosed that his campaign had paid him $163,000 for personal expenses from 1986 to 1990.

After he left office, Davis converted $40,147 in leftover campaign funds to personal use.

Business Address	*Home Address*
Bob Davis & Associates	2411 Belle Haven Meadows Court
2361 Jefferson Davis Highway 506	Alexandria, Virginia 22306
Arlington, Virginia 22202	(703) 765-3664
(703) 418-1410	

Senator Jeremiah Denton (R., Alabama)

Elected to the Senate in 1980, Denton served one term before he lost his 1986 reelection bid to then-Democrat Richard Shelby in a close and expensive race.

A Navy Admiral, Denton was held as a prisoner of war in North Vietnam for seven years, and while being filmed, blinked out the word 'torture' in Morse code. He was the first POW to return from North Vietnam and has been hailed as an authentic American hero.

Denton founded the National Forum Foundation in Washington, a nonprofit organization that aims to promote national defense. His son, Jim, now runs the organization. Today, Denton lives in Theodore, Alabama.

Business Address	*Home Address*
Denton Associates	Route 1, Box 305
1140413 Queens Way	Theodore, Alabama 36582
Theodore, Alabama 36582	

Representative Michael Dewine (R., Ohio)

Dewine was elected to the House in 1982 and served until 1990, when he was elected lieutenant governor of Ohio. In 1992, he challenged Democratic Senator John Glenn but was defeated. In 1994, he again ran for the Senate to fill the seat being vacated by Democratic Senator Howard Metzenbaum and he won the Republican primary in June. He defeated Democrat Joel Hyatt, Metzenbaum's son-in-law, in the November election.

Business Address
Lieutenant Governor
77 South High Street
30th Floor
Columbus, Ohio 43266
(614) 466-3396

Representative William Dickinson (R., Alabama)

Elected to the House in 1964, Dickinson retired in 1992 after a series of alleged ethical improprieties made his reelection outlook bleak. As the ranking Republican on the Armed Service Committee, Dickinson reportedly solicited $300,000 from a defense and textile manufacturing executive to invest in Montgomery Investment Club. "Dickinson was to receive one-third of the profits from the investment despite putting in no money of his own, but he got nothing when the investment turned out to be fraudulent," *Roll Call* reported in 1992.

Today, Dickinson runs a Capitol Hill consulting firm and splits his time between Alabama and Washington. When he left office, he converted approximately $55,104 in leftover campaign funds to personal use, including payments for office furniture, the purchase of a computer, payments on a Chrysler Imperial, travel expenses, auto insurance, and a $17,500 lump-sum salary payment to his wife, Barbara. He still has $319,312 remaining in his campaign account.

Business Address
The Dickinson Group
412 First Street, S.E. #60
Washington, D.C. 20003
(202) 488-1938

Home Address
2350 Woodley Road
Montgomery, Alabama 36111
and
3535 North Glebe Road
Arlington, Virginia 22202
(703) 241-8326

Representative Joseph DioGuardi (R., New York)

DioGuardi was elected to the House in 1984 as the only practicing Certified Public Accountant ever elected to Congress. He lost the 1988 election to Democrat Nita Lowey. The author of *Unaccountable Congress -- It Doesn't Add Up*, published by Regnery Gateway, DioGuardi has also produced a videotape about government spending titled: *The Most Expensive Credit Card in the World*.

"Congress is unaccountable -- it doesn't add up," DioGuardi says. "I'm trying to teach my kids that less [salary] is more. I'm spending all of my time writing." He also chairs Truth in Government, an organization that promotes fiscal integrity and honest accounting practices.

DioGuardi challenged Lowey in a rematch in 1992 and lost. In 1994, he ran for office again in an open seat created by the retirement of Representative Hamilton Fish, and lost.

Home Address
50 Baraud Road
Scarsdale, New York 10583
(914) 472-3376

Senator Alan Dixon (D., Illinois)

Elected to the Senate in 1980, Dixon lost the 1992 Democratic primary to Carol Moseley-Braun. He now practices law in St. Louis, Missouri. "Just practicing law and trying to make a living, and I'm doing rather well," Dixon told *Roll Call* in 1993.

Dixon also plans to take on some lobbying clients now that his one-year ban is over. "On several occasions I had to decline things . . . It makes a substantial difference in things that you can do out there," Dixon told the *Minneapolis Star Tribune*.

In 1994, President Clinton appointed Dixon to be chairman of the Defense Base Closure Commission.

Business Address
Brian Cave Law Firm
211 North Broadway Street
#3600
St. Louis, Missouri 63102
(314) 259-2550

Home Address
7535 Claymont Court
Belleville, Illinois 62223
(618) 397-3050

Representative Brian Donnelly (D., Massachusetts)

Elected to the House in 1978, Donnelly retired in 1992 when his congressional district was eliminated in redistricting. In 1993, he decided against running for mayor of Boston and was considered to be named Ambassador to Ireland, but the post went to Jean Kennedy Smith. Donnelly did serve the Clinton Administration as an alternate representative to the United Nations General Assembly in 1993.

President Clinton, in June 1994, appointed Donnelly to be Ambassador to the Caribbean Republic of Trinidad and Tobago. "I think his congressional experience and his ready sense of the appropriate role of an ambassador make him a good choice," Mark Gearan, White House Communications Director told the *Boston Globe*. "And he has shown a real strong interest in serving in the administration."

Donnelly used $30,000 from his congressional campaign account to make donations to other political candidates. He has $726,710 remaining in his account.

Home Address
59 Clearwater Drive
Boston, Massachusetts 02126
(617) 298-0927

Senator Byron Dorgan (D, North Dakota)

Dorgan was elected to the House in 1980 and to the Senate, where he currently serves, in 1992.

Business Address
713 Hart Senate Office Building
Washington, D.C. 20510
(202) 224-2551

Representative Charles Douglas (R., New Hampshire)

A former state Supreme Court justice, Douglas was elected to the House in 1988 and served one term. He lost the 1990 election to Democrat Dick Swett, the son-in-law of Representative Tom Lantos (D., California). He has returned to New Hampshire, where he practices law.

Business Address
Douglas & Douglas
6 Loudon Road, Suite 502
Concord, New Hampshire 03301
(603) 226-1988

Home Address
14 Ridge Road
Concord, New Hampshire 03301
(603) 224-8499

Representative Wayne Dowdy (D., Mississippi)

Dowdy won a special election to the House on July 7, 1981 to fill the vacancy created when Republican Representative Jon Hinson resigned from the House. (Hinson was arrested in a House office building men's restroom in February 1981 and charged with attempted oral sodomy.) Dowdy left the House in 1988 to run for the Senate but lost to Republican Representative Trent Lott. He now practices law in Magnolia, Mississippi, and lives six miles away in McComb. A successful businessman, Dowdy also owns several radio stations in the area. His assistant said that she couldn't remember him ever traveling to Washington.

Business Address
P.O. Box 30
Magnolia, Mississippi 39652
(601) 783-6600

Representative Thomas Downey (D., New York)

Elected to the House in 1974, Downey was defeated in the 1992 election after he had 151 overdrafts at the House bank where his wife, Chris, had once worked as an auditor.

Now a Washington lobbyist, Downey is the president of Downey Chandler, Inc.. The firm's clients have included the Breakthrough Technology Institute; the Center on Law and Social Policy; E.I. duPont de Nemours & Company; Joseph E. Seagram & Sons; Medco Containment Services, Inc.; Metropolitan Life and Affiliates; Monitor Aerospace Corporation; Time-Warner, Inc.; United Feather and Down; and U.S. Healthcare.

Downey converted $14,996 in leftover campaign funds to his personal use. He has $32,239 remaining in the account.

Also see the chapter, "The Revolving Door."

Business Address
Downey Chandler, Inc.
1401 I Street, N.W.
Suite 1210
Washington, D.C. 20005
(202) 898-6458

Representative John Duncan (R., Tennessee)

Elected to the House in 1964, Duncan died in office on June 21, 1988. His estate received $605,252 in leftover campaign funds and distributed the money to his widow and four children.

Representative Bernard Dwyer (D., New Jersey)

Elected to the House in 1980, Dwyer retired in 1992. He returned to New Jersey, where he is the chairman of Frazier Brothers Insurance.

Dwyer donated $54,986 in leftover congressional campaign funds to other political candidates and gave $43,900 to various organizations.

Business Address
Frazier Brothers Insurance
P.O. Box 2128
Edison, New Jersey 08818
(908) 738-7400

Home Address
31 Mason Drive
Edison, New Jersey 08820
(908) 548-4833

Representative Mervyn Dymally (D., California)

Elected to the House in 1980, Dymally retired in 1992 and returned to California, where he started Dymally International Group, Inc.. He is also involved in a consulting business with former Representative Jim Bates (D., Calif.).

Business Address
President
Dymally International Group, Inc.
9111 South LaCienega Boulevard
#201
Inglewood, California 90301
(310) 641-3688

Representative Roy Dyson (D., Maryland)

Elected to the House in 1980, Dyson lost the 1990 election to Republican Wayne Gilchrest after facing years of charges of various ethics violations. He worked in his family's hardware store in his hometown of Great Mills, Maryland and in 1994 won a seat in the Maryland State Senate.

Also see chapter "Hard Feelings: Roy Dyson."

Business Address
Dyson Building Center
Route 5
Great Mills, Maryland 20634
(301) 994-9000

Home Address
Route 5
Great Mills, Maryland 20634
(301) 944-0732

Senator Thomas Eagleton (D., Missouri)

Elected to the Senate in 1968, Eagleton retired from elective office in 1986 and returned to St. Louis. "In addition to practicing law at Thompson & Mitchell, I am university professor of public affairs at Washington University in St. Louis," he told us. In 1993, President Clinton appointed me to the President's Foreign Intelligence Advisory Board."

Eagleton gained national fame in 1972 when George McGovern, the Democratic presidential nominee, named him as his running mate. Shortly thereafter, it was disclosed that Eagleton had undergone electroconvulsive therapy for depression years before, and McGovern dropped him from the ticket.

Business Address
Thompson & Mitchell
Attorneys at Law
One Mercantile Center
St. Louis, Missouri 63101-1693
(314) 231-1717

Representative Joseph Early (D., Massachusetts)

Elected to the House in 1974, Early was defeated in 1992 by Republican Peter Blute after it was disclosed that Early had 140 overdrafts at the House Bank. He told *National Journal* in 1993 that he is doing "a little public relations work."

Business Address
36 Monroe Avenue
Worcester, Massachusetts 01601
(508) 752-6718

Senator John East (R., North Carolina)

Elected to the Senate in 1980, East died in office on June 29, 1986.

Representative Dennis Eckart (D., Ohio)

Elected to the House in 1980, Eckart retired in 1992 to become a Washington lobbyist. Eckart, who'd been a member of the powerful Energy and Commerce Committee, Eckart immediately joined the Washington office of Winston & Strawn, a Chicago-based law firm, after he left office. In 1994, he jumped to the Washington office of Arter & Hadden, a Cleveland-based law firm.

Eckart cited family reasons for leaving Congress. "Both my son and my father are growing older," Eckart told *The Washington Post*. "I am missing days with both."

Eckart has been described as young, smart and ambitious. "His potential has not even begun to be tapped," Tony Coelho told *National Journal*. "there are not many people like him at his age, [44] with his ability and these connections. That is what makes him such a superstar."

Eckart's earnings have skyrocketed since he left office and are now estimated to be in the range of $500,000 a year. He has also moved into what he describes as a "spacious" new home. "I am doing better in three ways: one, financially; two, in terms of time for my family; three, in terms of time for myself," Eckart told the *Cleveland Plain Dealer*.

At Arter & Hadden, Eckart has represented such health care interests as the American Insurance Association, Girling Healthcare, and Merck & Company. He also represents, along with former members Jim Florio and Bob Kasten, the Association for Responsible Thermal Treatment, a group of seven hazardous waste incineration companies.

Eckart has also represented Jefferies & Company, Inc., a brokerage firm based in Los Angeles. Boyd Jefferies, its chairman, was a junk-bond trader and pleaded guilty in 1987 to two felony counts of securities law violations.

Arter & Hadden's clients have included the Can Manufacturers Institute; Cellular Telecommunications Industry Association; Circus Enterprises, Incorporated; Corning Inc.; Financial Guaranty Insurance Corporation; Hearst Corporation; National Association of Broadcasters; Sprint Corporation; Tesoro Petroleum Corporation, U.S. Long Distance Corporation; and Westinghouse Electric Corporation.

Eckart gave $185,000 in his leftover campaign funds to Kent State University. He also refunded $1,500 in contributions and made $23,500 in political contributions.

Business Address
Arter & Hadden
1801 K Street, N.W.
Suite 400K
Washington, D.C. 20006
(202) 775-7100

Representative Fred Eckert (R., New York)

Eckert, who was elected to the House in 1984, served one term before he was defeated in the 1986 election. Before his election, he had beem the U.S. ambassador to Fiji, Tonga, Tuvalu, and Kiribati. President Reagan appointed him as

Ambassador to the United Nations Agencies for Food and Agriculture in 1987. Eckert had returned to Washington, where he ran Eckert International, a lobbying firm that represented Festival Shipping and Tourist Enterprises, Ltd., and the government of Fiji and Tonga. Eckert has recently moved and left no forwarding address.

Representative Bob Edgar (D., Pennsylvania)

Elected to the House in 1974, he gave up his seat in 1986 to make an unsuccessful bid for the Senate. Edgar is a Methodist minister who was an active opponent of the Vietnam war. Today, he is the president of the School of Theology at Claremont College in California.

Edgar says that he sees three challenges for theological education: "One, to internationalize ministry with a worldview responsive to changing realities. Two, to respond to the 'older generation' of theological students who come to ministry as a second career. And three, to help educate community leadership for Asian-American, African-American, and Hispanic-America churches."

Business Address   *Home Address*
School of Theology at Claremont College   1058 Cascade Place
125 North College Avenue   Claremont, California 91711
Claremont, California 91711   (909) 624-8224
(909) 626-3521

Representative Jack Edwards (R., Alabama)

Elected to the House in 1965, Edwards retired from office in 1984. He is now a partner in the law firm of Hand, Arendall, Bedsole, Greaves & Johnston. A registered lobbyist, he splits his time between Hand, Arendall's offices in Mobile, Alabama, and Washington.

Edwards has served as the chairman of the Mobile Area Chamber of Commerce and as a director of the Mobile Opera and the Mobile Economic Development Council, among other organizations. He was named Alabama's Volunteer Industrial Developer in 1987. In 1988, he was the co-chairman of the Defense Secretary's Commission on Base Realignment and Closure.

Edwards is now a director of Dravo Corporation, Holnam, Inc., Northrop Corporation, and The Southern Company.

Business Address   *Home Address*
Hand Arendall Bedsole, Greaves & Johnston   P.O. Box 380
P.O. Box 123   Point Clear, Alabama 36564
Mobile, Alabama 36601   (202) 928-1013
(205) 432-5511

Hand Arendall Bedsole, Greaves & Johnston
1667 K Street, N.W.
Suite 310
Washington, D.C. 20006
(202) 863-0053

and 110 D Street, S.E.
Washington, D.C. 20003
(202) 547-4398

Representative Mickey Edwards (R., Oklahoma)

Elected to the House in 1976, Edwards served until his defeat in the 1992 Republican primary. Edwards is now a lecturer in public policy at the John F. Kennedy School of Government at Harvard University. Edwards recently defended Congress with some tough comments about Republican Whip Newt Gingrich, saying that Gingrich's strategy can be "counterproductive."

"It has managed to destroy public confidence in government institutions," Edwards told *USA Today*. "And it hasn't meant more Republicans getting elected." This was said prior to November 8, 1994.

Edwards refunded all of his $19,186 in leftover campaign funds.

Business Address
Harvard University
79 John F. Kennedy Street
Cambridge, Massachusetts 02138?
(617) 496-3484

Representative Glenn English (D., Oklahoma)

English was elected to the House in 1974. In December 1993, just one month after he had successfully guided the elctrical cooperative's program through Congress, he resigned to become vice president and general manager of the National Rural Electrical Cooperative Association.

English was the chariman of the Agriculture Subcommittee on Environment, Credit, and Rural Development.

Business Address
National Rural Electrical Cooperative Association
1800 Massacusetts Avenue, NW
Washington, D.C. 20036
(202) 857-9500

Representative Ben Erdreich (D., Alabama)

Elected to the House in 1982, Erdreich lost the 1992 election to Republican Spencer Bachus. In July 1993, President Clinton appointed him to be the chairman of the U.S. Merit Systems Protection Board, a government agency that oversees the civil service system and federal employee rights. "After serving 10 years in Congress, President Clinton appointed me to chair this agency, a transition from elective office which I have very much enjoyed," Erdreich said.

Business Address	*Home Address*
Merit Systems Protection Board	2706 36th Street, N.W.
1120 Vermont Avenue, N.W.	Washington, D.C. 20007
Washington, D.C. 20419	
(202) 653-7101	

Representative John Erlenborn (R., Illinois)

Elected to the House in 1964, Erlenborn retired from elective office in 1984. He stayed in Washington and joined the Washington law firm of Seyfarth, Shaw, Fairweather and Geraldson, where he is of counsel.

At age 66, Erlenborn says that he is beginning the retirement process: "I'm getting to the point where I'm slowing down. I get back there [Illinois] occasionally; I still have family and friends there. I figure at my age, I can slow down to four days a week."

Retirement from the House proved to be tougher than Erlenborn had expected. "It was much more difficult than I thought, frankly," he said. "To quote a friend whose husband had left the Administration and returned to private law practice, 'When you're in public life, other people and outside events drive your schedule; when you leave, and go back to the practice of law, nothing happens until you make it happen.'"

An expert on employee benefit legislation in Congress, Erlenborn said that he practices benefit law and testifies as an expert witness in court cases. He also lobbies Congress for Unisys Corporation on health care issues.

Erlenborn and his wife have built a home on the Potomac River in Charles County, Maryland, where they spend their weekends. During the week they live in a Washington condominium.

Business Address
Seyfarth, Shaw, Fairweather and Geraldson., P.A.
815 Connecticut Avenue, N.W.
Suite 500
Washington, D.C. 20006
(202) 828-5333

Representative Mike Espy (D., Mississippi)

Elected to the House in 1986 as the first black congressman from Mississippi, Espy was appointed Secretary of Agriculture in 1992 by President-elect Clinton. Espy had 191 overdrafts at the House Bank.

In early 1994, it was disclosed that Espy had accepted free airplane rides and other gifts from Tyson Foods, a company that Espy's department regulated. He resigned as Agriculture Secretary on October 3, 1994. His mail will be forwarded.

Business Address
Department of Agriculture
Room 200
12th and Jefferson Drive, S.W.
Washington, D.C. 20250
(202) 720-3631

Representative Cooper Evans (R., Iowa)

Elected to the House in 1980, Evans retired in 1986. He founded Evans & Associates, an agricultural consulting business based in his hometown of Grundy Center, Iowa.

In 1989, President Bush appointed Evans as his special assistant for agricultural trade and food assistance, and he served in that capacity for two years. Out of politics, Evans started a horticultural farm in Missouri and a new calf-cow operation, in addition to his grain farm and walnut plantation, in Grundy Center. A popular agricultural speaker, he was recently the guest speaker at "Farmers for the Next Century: The First National Conference for Beginning Farmers and Ranchers" in Omaha, Nebraska. "We need to make a real incentive for the established farmer who's ready to get out of the business to convey his land to a beginning farmer, rather than to the largest landowner in the county," Evans said. "There are really many innovative ways government could facilitate succession if it wished to do so."

Evans gave all of his $30,148 in leftover campaign funds to other political candidates.

Home Address
1009 H. Avenue
Grundy Center, Iowa 50638
(319) 824-6451

Senator Daniel Evans (R., Washington)

Evans was appointed to the Senate on September 12, 1983 to fill the vacancy created by the death of Democrat Henry "Scoop" Jackson. Evans subsequently won reelection, but retired from the Senate in 1988. Evans had been a popular three-term governor in Washington and was the president of Evergreen College when he was appointed to the Senate.

Today, Evans is a busy speaker and radio and television commentator in Seattle. He has also been named to an advisory group at the Pacific Northwest Laboratory in Richland, Washington.

Business Address
KIRO-TV
1111 Third Avenue
Suite 3400
Seattle, Washington 98101
(206) 447-4700

Representative Dante Fascell (D., Florida)

Elected to the House in 1954, Fascell, chairman of the Foreign Affairs Committee, retired in 1992. He returned to Miami, where he works for the law firm of Holland and Knight.

"After eight years with the legislature of Florida, four as a state representative from Dade County, and 38 years in the U.S. House of Representatives, I decided to leave public life," Fascell says.

"My years in public service were a great challenge for me, my wife, my children, and our families. It meant many sacrifices for them, so I was fortunate to have their love and support.

"Public service was also a great honor for us despite it's manifest inconveniences. As someone once said, 'Democracy is not a spectator sport.' I am proud to say our families participated fully for 46 years, and we are still doing it, although from a slightly different vantage point.

"I maintain a strong interest in the foreign affairs of our country. I am associated with the Center for Strategic and International Studies as a senior counselor and as a member of the Council of Foreign Affairs. Serving as a member of the Committee on Foreign Affairs and then as its chairman, my initial interest in the world was sufficiently whetted for me to continue my interest and concern.

"I also continue to be deeply involved in community activities. I worked with the community effort to restore our community after Hurricane Andrew, with the organization We Will Rebuild. I am state chair of Kids Voting, an organization which instills the concept and process of voting in school children from kindergarten to 12 years of age as fundamental to a democratic system. I also participate in many other community organizations, in the fields of trade, commerce, development, health, and the environment.

"The work for Save the Everglades, complete acquisition for Biscayne National Park, Big Cypress Swamp, Florida Bay, and completing the regime for the Coral Reef National Preserve, all command a good part of my interest and concern.

"Today, I am back in the practice of law with the firm of Holland & Knight, with offices in Washington, Atlanta, and throughout Florida. It is the largest law firm in Florida, has a very realistic global reach, and serves client needs on every continent. I am very comfortable and content being part of their international and governmental division."

Fascell refunded $61,535 in leftover campaign funds and contributed $11,887 to other political candidates. He donated $100,000 to the University of Miami and $50,000 to the Miami Children's Hospital Foundation. He converted $41,153 of the campaign funds to personal use for payments to consultants and has $144,406 remaining in his account.

Business Address
Holland & Knight
P.O. Box 015441
Miami, Florida 33101
(305) 374-8500

Home Address
6300 S.W. 99th Terrace
Miami, Florida 33156

Representative Walter Fauntroy (D., District of Columbia)

Elected to the House in a 1971 special election, Fauntroy gave up his seat in 1990 to wage an unsuccessful campaign for mayor of Washington. He is now the president of Fauntroy & Associates and a registered lobbyist. Fauntroy has represented the African National Congress and organized the 30th anniversary commemoration of the March on Washington.

Business Address
Fauntroy & Associates
1025 Connecticut Avenue, N.W
Suite 610
Washington, D.C. 20036
(202) 296-0250

Representative Edward Feighan (D., Ohio)

Elected to the House in 1982, Feighan retired in 1992 after he had 397 overdrafts at the House bank to join the Cleveland law firm of Climaco, Climaco,

Seminatore, Lefkowitz & Garofoli. The law firm is a registered lobbyist for Blue Cross and Blue Shield of Ohio and Carbon Fuels Corporation of Cleveland.

Feighan started American Foreign Capital Partners, which represents Russian business interests, with Dan Clark, a former congressional aide. Feighan also is the co-owner of an Ohio micro-brewery that produces Erin Brew.

"I've had a wonderful year, beyond my best expectations," Feighan told the *Cleveland Plain Dealer* in January 1994. "It has been wonderful to come back and find out what a great job my wife did raising our children over the past 10 years."

With his former administrative assistant now a top adviser to President Clinton, Feighan's wife presented him with a Christmas gift membership to the George Stephanopoulos Fan Club.

Feighan converted $32,221 in leftover campaign funds to personal use, including $10,648 for office furniture and equipment and $12,573 for legal fees. He also made $76,550 in contributions to other political candidates and still has $55,088 in his campaign account.

Business Address
Climaco, Climaco, Seminatore, Lefkowitz & Garofoli
1228 Euclid Avenue
Cleveland, Ohio 44115
(216) 621-8484

Representative Geraldine Ferraro (D., New York)

Elected to the House in 1978, Ferraro gave up her seat to become Walter Mondale's running mate in the 1984 presidential campaign. In 1992, she ran for the Senate but was defeated in the Democratic primary.

Ferraro is a delegate to the U.N. World Conference of Human Rights and a partner in the New York law firm of Keck, Mahin & Cate. She represents the American Association for Marriage and Family Therapy on health care issues. "We hear from her all the time on health care," a senior aide to a Republican on the House Ways and Means Committee was reported saying.

She converted $20,405 in leftover campaign funds for personal use and spent $67,000 for a Senate exploratory committee in 1986.

Business Address
Keck, Mahin & Cate
220 East 42nd Street
New York, N.Y. 10017
(212) 490-3918

Representative Bobbi Fiedler (R., California)

Elected to the House in 1980, Fiedler gave up her seat to make an unsuccessful run for the Senate in 1986. Today, she lives in Northridge, California, with her husband, Paul Clarke. In 1993, she was appointed to a two-year term on the Los Angeles Community Redevelopment Agency.

"She's served her time, she's been paroled," Clarke said when asked about Fiedler's possible return to elective politics. "She's working on being the world's best grandmother."

Business Address
Community Redevelopment Agency
354 South Spring Street
Los Angeles, California 90013
(213) 977-1600

Representative Ronnie Flippo (D., Alabama)

Elected to the House in 1976, Flippo gave up his seat in 1990 to mount an unsuccessful campaign for governor of Alabama. Now, as a Washington-based lobbyist, his clients include the state of Alabama.

"The Cold War is over, defense expenses are being reduced, and the private sector is being beefed up," Flippo told States News Service in 1994. "The governor and delegation are just trying to position the state to participate and compete well in this new global economy that is an information-based economy."

Flippo's other clients have included Alabama Power Corporation, Federal Express Corporation, the Huntsville Madison County Airport Authority, Massachusetts Mutual Life Insurance Company, Norfolk Southern Corporation, RJR Nabisco, South Central Bell, and Troy State University.

Flippo has $485,009 in campaign funds still available. Since 1991, he has made $47,200 in political contributions, including $27,850 to 35 members of Congress during the 1992 election cycle.

Business Address
R.G. Flippo & Associates
701 Pennsylvania Avenue, N.W.
Suite 800
Washington, D.C. 20004
(202) 508-4397

Representative James Florio (D., New Jersey)

Elected to the House in 1974, Florio left Congress on January 1, 1990, after he was elected governor of New Jersey. He lost his 1993 reelection bid to Republican Christine Todd Whitman.

Florio is now a partner in the law firm of Mudge Rose Guthrie Alexander and Ferdon, where he advises clients on environmental, transportation, and trade issues. He also is teaching a course in the Fall of 1994 on decision making in the 1990s at Rutgers University, where he is professor for public policy and planning.

Florio is a director of Bally Gaming International and the Dehere Foundation and is the national chairman of the Transit NOW, a Washington-based mass transit advocacy group. Secretary of Labor Robert Reich named Florio to be the co-chair of the Task Force on Excellence in State and Local Government Through Labor-Management Cooperation. He is also a member of the U.S. Trade Representative's Investment and Services Policy Advisory Committee (INSPAC).

"In some instances, there is the capability of exerting positive influence on public policy more effectively from the outside," Florio told the *Bergen Record*. "You don't have the full scope of authority as you did on the inside. But there is the ability to marshall resources, to focus, and to get things done."

Florio also represents, along with former Republicans Dennis Eckart and Bob Kasten, the Association for Responsible Thermal Treatment, a group of seven hazardous waste incineration companies.

Business Address
Mudge Rose Guthrie Alexander and Ferdon
Morris Corporate Center Two
1 Upper Pond Road - Building D
Parsippanny, New Jersey 07054
(201) 335-0004

Representative Edwin Forsythe (R., New Jersey)

Forsythe, who was elected to the House in 1970, died in office on March 29, 1984. His estate received $41,259 in leftover campaign funds.

Senator Wyche Fowler (D., Georgia)

Fowler was elected to the House on April 5, 1977 in a special election to fill the vacancy created when Andrew Young left the House to become the U.S. Representative to the United Nations. Elected to the Senate in 1986, he was defeated in a 1992 general election runoff by Republican Paul Coverdell.

After his defeat, Fowler was appointed to the Federal Election Commission as the Senate's 'special deputy.' Fowler said that his task at the FEC was to develop campaign finance reform but he had little defined duties. In 1993, Fowler told Knight Ridder News Service that he was angered by reports that he had received special treatment for his appointment. "Why would I be down here?" he said. "You can't believe the amount of money I've been offered if I would go lobby my colleagues."

Apparently Fowler decided to lobby his colleagues, because he left the FEC in late 1993 to join the Washington office of the Atlanta law firm of Powell, Goldstein, Frazier & Murphy as a partner. The firms's clients have included British Airways, the Coalition for Diversified Gas Supplies, Dow Chemical, Dr Pepper, Esco Energy, Hewlett Packard, Hong Kong Trade Development Council, International Telephone & Telegraph Satellite Organization, Koyo Corp of USA, Lockheed, National Association of Public Hospitals, Nova Care, PSI Energy, Schering-Plough, and Uruguay Gas Transmission System, Vest Energy.

Business Address
Powell, Goldstein, Frazier & Murphy
1001 Pennsylvania Avenue, N.W.
#600 South
Washington, D.C. 20004
(202) 347-0066

Representative Webb Franklin (R., Mississippi)

Elected to the House in 1982, Franklin served until he lost the 1986 election to Democrat Mike Espy. Franklin returned home to Mississippi where he says that he is still heavily involved in local and state politics.

"I'm trying to pay all of the bills I accumulated in Congress," Franklin joked. "My wife would shoot me if I ran again."

Now a lawyer in Greenwood, Mississippi, Franklin says that he does state government relations work with agricultural clients and has done some limited work with some federal agencies on behalf of clients.

Home Address
P.O. Box 1176
Greenwood, Mississippi 38930
(601) 453-6576

Representative Bill Frenzel (R., Minnesota)

Elected to the House in 1971, Frenzel retired in 1992. "I serve on some do-gooder boards and make a few speeches for fees," he said. Frenzel lives in the

Washington suburb of McLean, Virginia, in the house he bought when he first went to Congress 23 years ago. He says that he makes it back to Minnesota about once a month.

When President Clinton was looking for congressional help to pass the North American Free Trade Agreement, he enlisted Frenzel to lobby for its approval. "They needed a Republican and they have chosen me," Frenzel said.

To work for the White House, Frenzel took a leave of absence from his position as a guest scholar at the Brookings Institution. Frenzel was a member of the Ways and Means Committee and was a frequent participant in trade meetings around the globe.

He says that he and his wife, Ruthy, are the "parents of three daughters and grandparents of two perfect grandchildren."

Frenzel gave all of his $184,990 in leftover campaign funds to other political organizations.

Business Address	*Home Address*
The Brookings Institution	6310 Stoneham Lane
1775 Massachusetts Avenue, N.W.	McLean, Virginia 22101
Washington, D.C. 20036	(703) 356-2898
(202) 797-6086	

Representative Don Fuqua (D., Florida)

Elected to the House in 1962, Fuqua retired in 1986 to become the president of the Aerospace Industries Association of America, a Washington-based lobbying organization. In the House, Fuqua was the chairman of the House Science and Technology Committee and its Energy Development and Applications Subcommittee.

In 1994, Fuqua lobbied the House to close down a number of military maintenance depots and let private firms that are members of his association contract for the repair business. Some members of the House Armed Services Committee objected to the plan. Fuqua told the *Sacramento Bee* that members of the House "think they're preserving something and they are not -- The Department of Defense will be forced to put some of these on the [closure] list."

Fuqua gave away all of his leftover campaign funds, including a $101,500 gift to Florida State University.

Business Address	*Home Address*
Aerospace Industries Association	3904 North Glebe Road
1250 I Street, N.W.	Arlington, Virginia 22207
11th Floor	(703) 237-0208
Washington, D.C. 20005	
(202) 371-8501	

Senator Jake Garn (R., Utah)

Elected to the Senate in 1974, Garn retired in 1992. Garn gained national fame in 1985 when he became the first member of Congress to ride on the space shuttle Discovery. His shuttle assignment was to test the effects of motion sickness while in space. Garn was the chairman of the Appropriations subcommittee that presided over NASA's budget.

A longtime critic of the way Congress does business, Garn said on the Senate floor in 1990 that "The Founding Fathers did not intend that we stay in session from January until December every year."

After he left the Senate, he returned to Salt Lake City and became the vice president of Huntsman Chemical Corporation.

Business Address
Huntsman Chemical Corporation
2000 Eagle Gate Tower
Salt Lake City, Utah 84111
(801) 532-5200

Representative Robert Garcia (D., New York)

Elected to the House in 1978, Garcia and his wife, Jane Lee, were convicted in October 1989 of charges stemming from the Wedtech Corporation scandal. Garcia was found guilty of extorting a $20,000 loan from a Wedtech executive, and Jane Lee Garcia was convicted of taking $76,000 in illegal consulting fees from the firm. He resigned from the House in January 1990.

In a 1992 interview with *Roll Call*, Garcia said that he was innocent of the charges but guilty of "stupidity."

"I just want my colleagues to know how terribly sorry I am for embarrassing them," Garcia said. Ironically, Garcia claimed in the 1992 interview that if he had known about the flexible House bank rules, he would have never gotten into trouble.

"The reason that all this came about was because I had to borrow money for an overdraft that my wife had and that I really didn't have enough time to go to the bank to borrow it," he said.

"I covered the sergeant-at-arms account with overdrafts from other banks. I never knew about the sergeant-at-arms. I always treated it as 'No way you could be overdrawn.' And yet I was overdrawn in New York. But I paid at least $15 a shot in New York."

Garcia served 104 days in prison before his conviction was reversed on appeal. A later trial found him guilty again, but the judge ordered no additional jail time. His wife received a three-month sentence.

Back in his old Bronx neighborhood, Garcia, who became active in Charles Colson's Prison Fellowship while serving his time, said that he works to promote the congressional members prayer breakfast and Bible study group.

Garcia used $146,969 in campaign funds for his 1989 legal bills.

Representative Joseph Gaydos (D., Pennsylvania)

Gaydos, who was elected to the House in 1968, retired in 1992 and started his own law firm, Gaydos & Gaydos.

Gaydos converted $98,500 in leftover campaign funds to personal use, refunded $1,500, and spent $949 for the "purchase of hams for political distribution."

Business Address
Gaydos & Gaydos
1223 Long Run Road
White Oak, Pennsylvania 15131
(412) 678-7900

Senator Barry Goldwater (R., Arizona)

Elected to the Senate in 1952, Goldwater served until he left to run as the Republican presidential nominee in 1964. He was elected again to the Senate in 1968 and served until he retired in 1986.

Today, Goldwater lives in Scottsdale, Arizona, where he is a popular political writer. He has recently taken on the cause of gay and lesbian rights.

"The conservative movement is founded on the simple tenet that people have the right to live as they please, as long as they don't hurt anyone else in the process," he wrote in July 1994. "No one has ever shown me how being gay or lesbian harms anyone else," he wrote in an opinion editorial in July, 1994. "Gays and lesbians are a part of every American family. They should not be shortchanged in their efforts to better their lives and serve their communities. It's time America realized that there is no gay exemption in the right to 'life, liberty, and the pursuit of happiness' in the Declaration of Independence. Job discrimination against gays -- or anybody else -- is contrary to each of these founding principles.

"It's not going to be easy getting Congress to provide job protection for gays. Constitutional conservatives know that doing the right thing takes guts and foresight, but that's why we're elected, to make tough decisions that stand the test of time."

Home Address
P.O. Box 1601
Scottsdale, Arizona 85252

Senator Albert Gore, Jr. (D., Tennessee)

Elected to the House in 1976, Gore served until he was elected to the Senate in 1984. In 1988, Gore made an unsuccessful bid for the Democratic presidential nomination, and in 1992, he became Bill Clinton's running mate and was elected Vice President. His father, Albert Gore, Sr., also served in the Senate from Tennessee.

Business Address
Vice President of the United States
Old Executive Office Building
Washington, D.C. 20510
(202) 456-2326

Representative Bill Gradison (R., Ohio)

Elected to the House in 1974, Gradison left office on January 31, 1993, to become the president of the Health Insurance Association of America.

Gradison refunded $39,037 in campaign contributions and donated $208,100 in leftover campaign funds to other candidates.

See the chapter "The Revolving Door."

Business Address
Health Insurance Association of America
1025 Connecticut Avenue, N.W.
12th Floor
Washington, D.C. 20036
(202) 223-7801

Representative Phil Gramm (R., Texas)

Elected to the House as a Democrat in 1978, Gramm changed parties in 1983 and was elected to the Senate as a Republican in 1984.

Business Address
370 Russell Senate Office Building
Washington, D.C. 20510
(202) 224-2934

Representative Bill Grant (R., Florida)

Elected to the House in 1986, Grant switched parties in 1989. He lost the 1990 election to Democrat Pete Peterson and mounted an unsuccessful challenge to Senator Bob Graham in 1992.

Today, Grant's home base is in Tallahassee, Florida, but he spends most of his time on the road. He works for IBE, an international group of companies and barter businesses, and maintains offices in New York City and Africa.

Leaving public life was tough for Grant. "Yes, in many ways, it was hard," he said. "There is an exhilaration that goes with public life and while it's frustrating, it has its rewards."

It's a "hold-on-for-dear-life existence. The adjustment depends in many ways on how you left office. If you are not quite ready to leave, there is a part of you that is missing. I don't care who the person is, when you go into public life, you think, 'I can do something good.' Yeah, there's an adjustment period.

"I'm not like some people. I think it's our responsibility to be in politics. I think we ought to do as much as we can, whoever we are."

Business Address
IBE
950 Third Avenue
25th Floor
New York, New York 10022
(212) 593-3255

Representative Kenneth Gray (D., Illinois)

Elected to the House in 1954, Gray served for 20 years until a heart condition forced him to retire and move to Florida. Gray recovered, moved back to Illinois, and was again elected to the House in 1984 and served until he retired for good in 1988.

He founded and currently runs the Ken Gray Historical Museum in West Frankfort, Illinois.

Business Address
Ken Gray Historical Museum
R.R. #4, Box 61
West Frankfort, Illinois 62896
(618) 937-6100

Representative William Gray (D., Pennsylvania)

Elected to the House in 1978, Gray resigned in September 1991, to become the president and CEO of the United Negro College Fund. In 1994, President Clinton named Gray to be his special adviser on Haiti.

Business Address
United Negro College Fund
700 13th Street, N.W.
Suite 1180
Washington, D.C. 20005
(202) 737-8623

Representative Judd Gregg (R., New Hampshire)

Elected to the House in 1980, Gregg served until he was elected governor of New Hampshire in 1988. In 1992, after his gubernatorial term was over, he was elected to the Senate.

Business Address
393 Russell Senate Office Building
Washington, D.C. 20510
(202) 224-3324

Representative Bill Green (R., New York)

Elected to the House in a special election on February 14, 1978, Green served until he was defeated by Democrat Carolyn Maloney in the 1992 election. He returned to New York City where he is an active member of various corporate boards, including Clientsoft, a computer software developer; Energy Answers Corporation, a resource recovery company firm; the General American Investors Company, a closed-end investment company; and the New York City Housing Development Corporation.

Business Address
14 East 60th Street
New York, New York 10022
(212) 755-6528

Home Address
755 Park Avenue
New York, New York 10021

Representative John Grotberg (R., Illinois)

Elected to the House in 1984, Grotberg died in office on November 15, 1986.

Representative Frank Guarini (D., New Jersey)

Elected to the House in 1978, Guarini retired in 1992 and returned to his hometown of Jersey City, New Jersey. Guarini says that he is catching up with his family and enjoying a little more "space and time and making up for 14 years that I've neglected."

As a senior partner in the law firm of Guarini & Guarini, he says that he is busy developing a government relations program for St. Peter's College in Jersey City. Guarini says that he will not do government relations work because he "considers that taking advantage of having a tour in Congress."

Guarini gave approximately $94,390 in leftover campaign funds to other political candidates and spent $243,326 on other items.

Business Address
Guarini & Guarini
Journal Square Plaza
Jersey City, New Jersey 07306
(201) 653-0050

Home Address
201 St. Paul's Avenue
Jersey City, New Jersey 07306
(201) 656-6377 or (201) 582-7197

Representative Katie Hall (D., Indiana)

Elected to the House in 1982, Hall was still in her first term when she lost the 1984 Democratic primary. She lives in Gary, Indiana.

Representative Sam Hall (D., Texas)

Elected to the House in a special election on June 19, 1976, Hall served until May 27, 1985, when President Reagan appointed him a federal judge. Hall died of a heart attack in April 1994. He converted $58,433 in leftover campaign funds to personal use after he left the House.

Representative John Paul Hammerschmidt (R., Arkansas)

Hammerschmidt, who was elected to the House in 1966, retired in 1992 after it was disclosed that he had 224 overdrafts at the House bank. He is working with the John Paul Hammerschmidt Business and Conference Center of North Arkansas Community College and the Twin Lake Technical College in Arkansas. He is also the chairman of the Northwest Arkansas Council, a not-for-profit organization that deals with infrastructure problems.

As a political footnote, in 1976 Hammerschmidt defeated an upstart young Democratic challenger named Bill Clinton.

Business Address
P.O. Box 989
Harrison, Arkansas 72610
(501) 743-2333

Representative Kent Hance (D., Texas)

Elected to the House in 1978, Hance gave up his House seat in 1984 to mount an unsuccessful campaign for the Senate. He switched political parties, and, in 1986, ran for governor but lost in the Republican primary. The eventual winner of the race, William Clements, appointed Hance to be the chairman of the Texas Railroad Commission, the powerful agency that regulates the oil, natural gas, rail and trucking industries in Texas.

In 1990, Hance again ran for governor of Texas, but lost the GOP primary to Clayton Williams. Today, he is a lobbyist with Hance and Gamble. His partner, J. Phillips Gamble, was Hance's counsel during his tenure on the railroad commission. The firm has offices in Austin and Washington.

"I started to go into pig farming but I didn't have enough money," Hance joked. "Wanted to upgrade. I'm living in Austin and do a lot of state and federal agency type work. Business is good. When you leave Congress, you substantially increase your pay and substantially decrease your hours."

Hance said that he is not interested in returning to elective office. "I've never gone back to repeat something I've already done. I think it [politics] is a mess. I feel sorry for everyone. It's gotten so that no matter what happens, everyone's going to yell. It's so partisan. It seems like the parties and the caucuses are more concerned about the next election than the future of the country."

Business Address
Hance and Gamble
400 West 15th Street
Suite 320
Austin, Texas 78701
(512) 479-8888

Representative George Hansen (R., Idaho)

Hansen was elected to the House in 1964 and served until he unsuccessfully challenged Democratic Senator Frank Church in 1968. Reelected to the House in

1974, Hansen lost the 1984 election after he was convicted in April 1984 of violating the 1978 Ethics in Government Act.

Hansen had failed to report nearly $334,000 in loans and profits that were in his wife's name. Connie Hansen, who worked as her husband's congressional assistant, was prosecuted for accepting a $50,000 unreported loan from Nelson Bunker Hunt and $87,000 in silver futures from a transaction made with Hunt's guidance. Hansen was sentenced to five to 15 months in prison and fined $40,000.

Today, Hansen is back in federal prison, serving a four-year sentence after he was convicted of defrauding five banks.

Representative Tom Harkin (D., Iowa)

Elected to the House in 1974, Harkin unseated Republican Senator Roger Jepsen in 1984. He was an unsuccessful candidate for the 1992 Democratic presidential nomination.

Business Address
531 Hart Senate Office Building
Washington, D.C. 20510
(202) 224-3254

Representative Frank Harrison (D., Pennsylvania)

Elected to the House in 1982, Harrison was still in his first term when he lost the 1984 Democratic primary.

Harrison could not be located.

Representative Claude Harris (D., Alabama)

Elected to the House in 1986, Harris retired in 1992. He was nominated by President Clinton and confirmed by the Senate to be the U.S. Attorney for the Northern District of Alabama.

Harris refunded $50,800 in campaign contributions, gave another $58,215 in leftover campaign funds to political candidates, and contributed $69,000 to other organizations.

Harris died of lung cancer on October 2, 1994.

Senator Gary Hart (D., Colorado)

Hart served two terms in the Senate, from 1974 to 1986. He was an unsuccessful candidate for the Democratic presidential nomination in 1984 and 1988. Hart now lives in Kittredge, Colorado, with his wife, Lee. He is a lawyer with the New York City-based law firm of Coudert Brothers. His latest book, *The Good Fight: The Education of an American Reformer*, was published in 1993 by Random House.

Business Address
Coudert Brothers
9785 Maroon Circle
Suite 210
Englewood, Colorado 80112
(303) 649-4656

Representative Thomas Hartnett (R., South Carolina)

Elected to the House in 1980, Hartnett gave up his seat in 1986 to run unsuccessfully for lieutenant governor of South Carolina. In 1992 he lost his challenge to Democratic Senator Ernest Hollings and in 1994 ran for governor but lost the Republican primary.

Business Address
Hartnett Realty Company
P.O. Box 221
Charleston, South Carolina 29401
(803) 723-7222

Representative Charles Hatcher (D., Georgia)

Hatcher was elected to the House in 1980. In 1992, after it was disclosed he'd had 819 overdrafts at the House bank, Hatcher was defeated by Sanford Bishop in the Democratic primary.

Home Address
P.O. Box 564
Alexandria, Virginia 22313

Representative Augustus Hawkins (D., California)

Elected to the House in 1962, Hawkins retired in 1990. He is currently living in Los Angeles.

Hawkins transferred $122,297 in leftover campaign funds to his personal account but told *Roll Call* in February 1993 that he did not intend to keep the money and was planning to give it to various foundations. He donated $20,000 to a neighborhood association in Los Angeles.

Home Address
3782 Hepburn Avenue
Los Angeles, California 90018

Senator Paula Hawkins (R., Florida)

Elected to the Senate in 1980, Hawkins was defeated by Democrat Bob Graham in the 1986 election. Currently a registered lobbyist, Hawkins's clients include the Pharmaceutical Research and Manufacturers of America.

Business Address
P.O. Box 193
Winter Park, Florida 32790
(407) 647-3498 or (407) 677-3020

Representative Charles Hayes (D., Illinois)

Elected to the House in a special election on September 12, 1983, Hayes lost the 1992 Democratic primary to Bobby Rush after it was disclosed that he had 716 overdrafts at the House bank. Hayes told *National Journal* in 1993 that he was planning on writing his memoirs and trying to raise money to retire his $50,000 campaign debt.

Senator Chic Hecht (R., Nevada)

Elected to the Senate in 1982, Hecht was defeated by Democrat Richard Bryan in 1988. In 1989, President Bush nominated him to be ambassador to the Bahamas. Hecht got into hot water after he was nominated when he said that he was looking forward to becoming ambassador because the islands offered gambling casinos, good golf and fishing. "I am sure I will feel at home in the Bahamas," he said. "I understand it's a nice lifestyle." He has now returned to his home in Las Vegas.

Home Address
47 Country Club Lane
Las Vegas, Nevada 98109
(702) 735-1286

Representative Cecil Heftel (D., Hawaii)

Heftel, who was elected to the House in 1976, gave up his seat in 1986 to mount an unsuccessful bid to be governor of Hawaii. Today, Heftel says that he spent "10 years accomplishing nothing." He currently is the owner and Chief Executive Officer of Heftel Broadcasting, KTNQ-KLVE in Los Angeles.

Business Address
Heftel Broadcasting
1645 North Vine Street
2nd Floor
Hollywood, California 90028
(213) 465-3171

Senator John Heinz (R., Pennsylvania)

Heinz, who was elected to the House in 1970 and to the Senate in 1976, was killed in a helicopter crash in April 1991 while in his third term.

Representative Bill Hendon (R., North Carolina)

Hendon was elected to the House in 1980, lost to Democrat James McClure Clarke in 1982, but then came back to defeat Clarke in 1984. Clarke, however, took the seat back in 1986.

As the director of the Washington-based POW Publicity Fund, Hendon works to secure the return of American prisoners of war. After leaving the House, Hendon says that he worked as a consultant on POWs for the Pentagon and as an investigator for the Senate Select Committee on POWs.

Business Address
POW Publicity Fund
P.O. Box 65500
Washington, D.C. 20035
(202) 686-4265

Representative Paul Henry (R., Michigan)

Elected to the House in 1984, Henry died in office in 1993.

Representative Dennis Hertel (D., Michigan)

Elected to the House in 1980, Hertel retired in 1992 after redistricting placed him in the same district as fellow Democratic Representative Sander Levin. Hertel also faced political trouble because he had 547 overdrafts at the House bank.

Hertel later founded his own law and lobbying group, Hertel & Associates, in Arlington, Virginia. Along with former Republican Representative Don Ritter, Hertel heads the National Environmental Policy Institute. The organization, which is financed by corporate interests, promotes environmental ideas that are "based on good science, rational risk assessment, and sound economics," according to a brochure.

Business Address	*Home Address*
Hertel & Associates	9721 Locusst Hill
2361 South Jefferson Davis Highway	Great Falls, Virginia 22006
Arlington, Virginia 22202	also
(703) 418-6880	20705 Woodside
	Harper Woods, Michigan 48225
	(703) 759-6572

Representative Jack Hightower (D., Texas)

Hightower, who was elected to the House in 1974, was unseated by Republican Beau Boulter in 1984. In 1988, he was elected to a six-year term as a justice of the Texas Supreme Court. Hightower, now 72, decided to retire in late 1994.

Hightower converted $14,057 in leftover campaign funds to his personal use.

Business Address	*Home Address*
Supreme Court of Texas	5905 Doone Valley Court
P.O. Box 12248	Austin, Texas 79731
Austin, Texas 78711	(512) 452-7327
(512) 463-1328	

Representative John Hiler (R., Indiana)

Elected to the House in 1980, Hiler was unseated in 1990 by Democrat Tom Roemer. President Bush then nominated him to head the General Services Administration. Hiler has now returned to Indiana and works in his family's business, Hiler Industries, which he says produces "shell mold castings in brass, bronze, aluminum, Gray and Ductile Iron."

Business Address	*Home Address*
Hiler Industries	1210 East Wayne Street
P.O. Box 639	South Bend, Indiana 46615
LaPorte, Indiana 46350	(219) 232-0985
(219) 362-8531	

Representative Elwood "Bud" Hillis (R., Indiana)

Elected to the House in 1970, Hillis retired in 1986 and returned to his former district. Today, he is a retired lawyer.

Home Address
176 South Shore Drive
Culver, Indiana 46511
(317) 459-3153

Representative Clyde Holloway (R., Louisiana)

Elected to the House in 1986, Holloway was unseated in 1992 by Democrat Richard Baker. He owns Clyde Holloway's Nursery in his hometown of Forest Hill, Louisiana.

Business Address
Clyde Holloway's Nursery
P.O. Box 339
Forest Hill, Louisiana 71430
(318) 748-6803

Representative Marjorie Holt (R., Maryland)

Elected to the House in 1972, Holt retired in 1986. President Reagan named her to the General Advisory Committee on Arms Control and Disarmament in July 1987 and she worked for a Baltimore law firm for three years after she left Congress practicing corporate law and screening clients. Now fully retired, Holt says that she lives in the same house where she "stayed all along" and has become "a pack rat."
Holt converted $60,743 in leftover campaign funds to personal use.

Home Address
151 Boone Trail
Severna, Maryland 21146
(410) 647-4288

Representative Larry Hopkins (R., Kentucky)

Elected to the House in 1978, Hopkins retired in 1992. President Clinton appointed him to the Agriculture Department's Tobacco Department Division in

1993, but Hopkins resigned after it was disclosed that he had converted $665,000 in leftover campaign funds to personal use.

Hopkins cannot be located.

Representative Joan Kelly Horn (D., Missouri)

Elected to the House in 1990, Horn lost the 1992 election to Republican James Talent. President Clinton appointed her to chair the Defense Department's Reinvestment Task Force and she says that she still commutes between Washington and St. Louis.

Business Address
Reinvestment Task Force
Office of the Assistant
 Secretary of Defense
 for Economic Security
Room 3E813, 3300 Defense
Washington, D.C. 20301
(703) 697-1771

Home Address
8570 Colonial Lane
St. Louis, Missouri 63124

Representative Frank Horton (R., New York)

Elected to the House in 1962, Horton retired in 1992. He is currently of counsel to the government division of the Washington law firm of Venable, Baetjer, Howard & Civiletti. The firm is a registered foreign agent and its clients have included Associated Builders and Contractors, International Mass Retail Association, the Mid-Atlantic Toyota Retail Association, the National Council of Juvenile and Family Court Judges, National Criminal Justice Association and the National Infomercial Marketing Association.

Horton converted $112,430 in leftover campaign funds to personal use. He told *Roll Call* in February 1993 that he planned to use some of the money to defray expenses that he incurred while in Congress. The remaining money, he said, would go to charities and scholarships. Horton also gave $7,000 in political contributions.

Business Address
Venable, Baetjer, Howard & Civiletti
1201 New York, Avenue, N.W.
Suite 1000
Washington,D.C. 20005
(202) 962-4956

Home   Address
3818 Poe Court
Annandale, Virginia 22003

Representative James J. Howard (D., New Jersey)

Elected to the House in 1964, Howard died in office on March 24, 1988. His widow received the $326,306 in leftover campaign funds.

Representative Carroll Hubbard (D., Kentucky)

Elected to the House in 1974, Hubbard was defeated in the 1992 Democratic primary by Tom Barlow after it was disclosed that he'd had 152 overdrafts at the House bank. He pleaded guilty in April 1994 to three felony charges resulting from the misuse of campaign funds and congressional staff and obstruction of justice. In November 1994, Hubbard was sentenced to three years in prison. His wife, Carol Brown Hubbard, was convicted of a misdemeanor for her role in the campaign and was sentenced to five years' probation, $27,000 in restitution and 100 hours of community service.

Hubbard, who converted $216,018 in leftover campaign funds to personal use, told *Roll Call* that he was using the money to pay off debts from his years in Congress. He also said that he would probably convert the $16,500 remaining in his campaign account to personal use.

Business Address
812 Freeman Lake Road
Elizabethtown, Kentucky 42701
(502) 737-3729

Representative Jerry Huckaby (D., Louisiana)

Elected to the House in 1976, Huckaby lost the 1992 election to Republican Representative Jim McCrery after redistricting pitted the two lawmakers in the same district. After leaving the House, Huckaby joined the Jefferson Group, a Washington lobbying firm, as a senior vice president. He later left the Jefferson Group and is now selling real estate in the Washington area.

In January 1994, Huckaby told Gannett News Service that he could be lured back into politics if his old seat were reinstated by the Supreme Court. "It would be a sacrifice for my family to run, but depending on what kind of district they draw, I would certainly look at it," Huckaby said. "It's great not having those pressures. I was one of those behind-the-scenes deal makers, if I might use that expression, and I tried to help put coalitions together, make things happen. And I miss that."

Home Address
6700 Sorrell Drive
McLean, Virginia 22101
(703) 734-0056

Senator Walter Huddleston (D., Kentucky)

Huddleston, who was elected to the Senate in 1972, lost the 1984 election to Republican Mitch McConnell. He is the senior vice president of Hecht, Spencer & Oglesby, Inc., a Washington lobbying firm.

Business Address
Hecht, Spencer & Oglesby, Inc.
499 South Capitol Street, S.W., Suite 507
Washington, D.C. 20003
(202) 544-2881

Senator Gordon Humphrey (R, New Hampshire)

Elected to the Senate in 1978, Humphrey retired in 1990, keeping his pledge to serve only two terms. "I was very tempted to run for a third term," Humphrey said. "But I finally decided I didn't want to spend my life in Washington making up excuses why I should run again."

Today, he lives in the same home in New Hampshire that he lived in while in the Senate. Humphrey runs his own consulting business, which works with U.S. companies that want to do business in Russia, and says that he spends about 10 days a month in his Moscow office.

"I didn't want to stay in Washington, and I didn't want to be a lobbyist," he said. "It seemed that this was a good way to earn a living and it combines business, economics, foreign policy, and promoting American exports. And it's even fairly lucrative."

Home Address
Garvin Hill Road
Trichester, New Hampshire 03301
(603) 798-5274

Representative Andy Ireland (R., Florida)

Elected to the House in 1976 as a Democrat, Ireland changed parties in 1984 and served until he retired in 1992. Ireland then took a job with the Jefferson Group, a Washington lobbying firm, but stayed only a few months. He is now the vice president of government relations for Irvin and Kenneth Feld Productions, Inc., which owns the Ringling Brothers Barnum & Bailey Circus.

Ireland gave $28,000 in leftover campaign funds to other political organizations, including $25,000 to the Florida Republican Party.

Business Address	*Home Address*
Irvin & Kenneth Feld Productions, Inc.	P.O. Box 2028
8607 Westwood Center Drive	Holmes Beach, Florida 34218
Vienna, Virginia 22182	(813) 778-5744
(703) 448-4090	

Representative Craig James (R., Florida)

Elected to the House in 1988, James retired in 1992 saying that he was frustrated with the institution. He has returned to his former law firm in his hometown of Deland, Florida. "I really enjoyed the issues, the participation, but I didn't enjoy Congress as an institution," James told the *Orlando Sentinel* in January 1994. "Every time I think I might miss it, I turn on C-SPAN and my level of frustration returns."

Business Address	*Home Address*
James, Zimmerman & Paul	245 East Shady Branch Trail
431 East New York Avenue	Deland, Florida 32724
Deland, Florida 32721	(904) 736-0832
(904) 734-1200	

Representative James Jeffords (R., Vermont)

Jeffords, who was elected to the House in 1974, was elected to the Senate in 1988 and reelected in 1994.

Business Address
513 Hart Senate Office Building
Washington, D.C. 20510
(202) 224-5141

Representative Ed Jenkins (D., Georgia)

Elected to the House in 1976, Jenkins retired in 1992. He set up the Washington-based lobbying firm of Winburn & Jenkins with John Winburn, his former congressional aide. The firm's clients have included Bell Atlantic Corporation, Burlington Northern Railroad, Leggett & Platt, Pennziol Company, Pfizer Corporation and the Philip Morris Management Company.

Business Address	*Home Address*
Winburn & Jenkins	202 Foxrun
50 E Street, S.E.	P.O. Box 70
Washington, D.C. 20003	Jasper, Georgia 30143
(202) 488-3581	(706) 692-2059

Senator Roger Jepsen (R., Iowa)

Elected to the Senate in 1978, Jepsen was unseated in 1984 by Democrat Tom Harkin. In 1985, President Reagan appointed him to be the chairman of the National Credit Union Administration, where he worked until his retirement in 1993.

Home Address
2987 Mission Square Drive
Fairfax, Virginia   22031
(703) 281-5341

Representative Ben Jones (D., Georgia)

Elected to the House in 1988, Jones served for two terms before he lost the 1992 Democratic primary to Don Johnson. The former television actor -- he played 'Cooter' on the "Dukes of Hazard" -- is a recovering alcoholic who now speaks regularly on the subject. He even hosted a radio call-in show in February 1994 called "The Second Chance Saloon."

In 1994, Jones rented an apartment back in Georgia, where he again ran unsuccessfully for the House against Republican Newt Gingrich. "I call the effort tilting at windbags," Jones told *The Washington Post*. "He's [Gingrich] running for a ninth term, and all he's interested in is the power. He's for term limits for everyone but himself. I'm not going to engage in the personal stuff. I read somewhere that Gingrich didn't have any comment on my running, and I thought, 'Amazing -- Gingrich struck dumb over Cooter!'"

Home Address
3887 Rodman Street, N.W.
Washington, D.C. 20016
(202) 537-4858

Representative Ed Jones (D., Tennessee)

Elected to the House in a special election on March 25, 1969, Jones retired in 1988. He started the lobbying firm of Cashdollar-Jones & Company, which has offices in Washington and Yorkville, Tennessee. "Being a conscientious and effective congressman was a grueling, demanding job," Jones says. "But I don't believe anyone has loved it any more than I did."

Jones converted $130,686 in leftover campaign funds to personal use. "The contributors didn't care what I did with [the fund]," Jones told the *Baltimore Sun* in February 1990. "I just decided to close the sucker out and be through with it."

Business Address
Cashdollar-Jones & Company
P.O. Box 128
Yorkville, Tennessee 38389
(901) 643-6400

Representative James Jones (D., Oklahoma)

Elected to the House in 1972, Jones was unseated in 1986 by Republican Don Nickles. After he left the House, Jones became the chairman and Chief Executive Officer of the American Stock Exchange and remained active in national politics. In 1993, President Clinton named him Ambassador to Mexico.

Business Address
Ambassador to Mexico
P.O. Box 3087
Laredo, Texas 78044

Representative Walter Jones (D., North Carolina)

Elected to the House in 1966, Jones died in office in 1992. His estate received all $270,000 in leftover campaign funds.

Representative Jim Jontz (D., Indiana)

Elected to the House in 1986, Jontz was unseated in 1992 by Republican Steven Buyer. In 1993, he became the director of the Citizens' Trade Campaign, a coalition working against the North American Free Trade Agreement. He unsuccessfully challenged Republican Senator Richard Lugar in 1994.

Senator David Karnes (R., Nebraska)

Karnes was appointed to the Senate on March 13, 1987 to fill the vacancy created by the death of Senator Edward Zorinsky. He lost the 1988 election to Democrat Bob Kerrey.

Today, Karnes is a lawyer with the Omaha-based firm of Kutak Rock. Karnes says that he gets to Kutak Rock's Washington office about eight to nine days a month. He still maintains some political involvement, and is the chairman of the 10th District Federal Home Loan Bank Board.

Karnes says that at this point in his life it is much easier leading a "normal" life in Omaha where he and his wife and four daughters are surrounded by their families and friends.

Business Address
Kutak Rock
1650 Farnam Street
Omaha, Nebraska 68102
(402) 346-6000

Senator Bob Kasten (R., Wisconsin)

Kasten was elected to the House in 1974 and to the Senate in 1980. He was unseated in 1992 by Democrat Russell Feingold.

Kasten is now the chairman on Regulation and Economic Growth, an adjunct of the Alexis de Tocqueville Institution in Arlington, Virginia. He is also the president of Kasten & Company, a Washington-based international business consulting firm.

"The federal government pays interest today because the Congress has spent more than it collected in taxes," he recently wrote in the *Washington Times*. "Many of the programs funded with borrowed money have indeed been wasteful, fraudulent, and abusive. Those programs, not the subsequent, inevitable interest payments, should be criticized."

Business Address
Kasten & Company
815 Connecticut Avenue, N.W.
Suite 800
Washington, D.C. 20002
(202) 223-9151

Representative Robert Kastenmeier (D., Wisconsin)

Elected to the House in 1958, Kastenmeier was unseated in 1990 by Republican Scott Klug.

See chapter "You Can't Go Home Again: Bob Kastenmeier"

Business Telephone Number
(202) 707-1555

Home Address
2800 North 27th Street
Arlington, Virginia 22207
(703) 525-7484

Representative Abraham Kazen (D., Texas)

Elected to the House in 1966, Kazen lost the 1984 Democratic primary to Albert Bustamante. He died while in office in November 1984.

Representative Jack Kemp (R., New York)

Elected to the House in 1970, Kemp gave up his seat in 1988 to run for President. Kemp served as Secretary of Housing and Urban Development in the Bush Administration and in 1993, founded Empower America.

Business Address
Empower America
1776 I Street, N.W.
8th Floor
Washington, D.C. 20006
(202) 452-8200

Representative Thomas Kindness (R., Ohio)

Kindness was elected to the House in 1974 and gave up his seat in 1986 to make an unsuccessful bid for the Senate. He again ran for the House in 1990 but lost the Republican primary to Jack Boehner after he was attacked for working as a Washington lobbyist.

Today, Kindness says that he is "busy trying to make a living, waiting for the economy to improve." As a lawyer and government affairs consultant with Kindness & Chatfield in Washington, Kindness says that most of his business involves legal work instead of lobbying.

Business Address
Kindness & Chatfield
1747 Pennsylvania Avenue, N.W.
Suite 1150
Washington, D.C. 20006
(202) 429-6060

Representative Ray Kogovsek (D., Colorado)

Elected to the House in 1978, Kogovsek retired in 1984. He is now a registered lobbyist and the president of Kogovsek & Associates, Inc. based in Denver, Colorado. His clients have included: the Amimas-Laplata Water Conservancy District; Blue Cross/Blue Shield of Colorado, New Mexico, and Nevada; the Dolores Water Conservancy District; the National Association of Counties; the Rio Grande Water Conservancy District; Shell Oil Company; the Southern Ute Indian Tribe; and the Ute Mountain Ute Indian Tribe.

Business Address	*Home Address*
Kogovsek & Associates, Inc.	8 Knightsbridge
700 Broadway	Pueblo, Colorado 81001
Suite 929	(719) 542-4272
Denver, Colorado 80203	
(303) 831-8400	

Representative Joe Kolter (D., Pennsylvania)

Elected to the House in 1982, Kolter was defeated by Ron Klink in the 1992 Democratic primary after he was implicated in the House Post Office scandal. He is currently under federal investigation following allegations that he misused House expense accounts to purchase personal items. Kolter was named, along with Representative Dan Rostenkowski, of Illinois, in federal subpoenas concerning the House Post Office, and the current investigation is part of a federal grand jury inquiry. Kolter allegedly used a House Post Office employee as a personal driver in 1990 and 1991. In November 1994, Kolter pleaded not guilty to charges related to the investigation.

Home Address
2185 Mercer Road
New Brighton, Pennsylvania 15066
(412) 846-3603

Representative Ernie Konnyu (R., California)

Elected to the House in 1986, Konnyu lost the 1988 Republican primary to Tom Campbell. Konnyu, who was accused of sexual harassment by a female aide, had the highest congressional staff turnover rate in 1987. He declined to discuss his current plans.

In 1994, Konnyu ran for assessor of Santa Clara County, California. In his campaign stationery, according to the *San Francisco Chronicle*, Konnyu bills himself as "The Honorable Ernest L. Konnyu, Former Member of Congress." The stationery includes a "cartoon of a big bear, Capitol dome perched on his head, chasing a crowd of fleeing people," the newspaper reported. "The bear is clutching a knife and fork and is salivating."

Business Address
Premier Printing & Communication
2362 Qume Drive, #F
San Jose, California 95131
(408) 434-6968

Representative Peter Kostmayer (D., Pennsylvania)

Elected to the House in 1976, Kostmayer lost his 1980 reelection bid but came back two years later to regain the seat. He lost the 1992 election to Republican Jim Greenwood. Kostmayer is now the Environmental Protection Agency's administrator for the middle Atlantic states.

Business Address	*Home Address*
Environmental Protection Agency, Region III	241 South 6th Street
841 Chestnut Street	Apartment 1709
Philadelphia, Pennsylvania 95131	Philadelphia, Pennsylvania 19106
(215) 597-9814	(215) 413-2136

Representative Ken Kramer (R., Colorado)

Elected to House in 1978, Kramer gave up his seat in 1986 to make an unsuccessful bid for the Senate. After a brief stint as Assistant Secretary of the Army for Financial Management, Kramer was nominated by President Reagan and confirmed by the Senate to a 15-year term as associate judge for the U.S. Court of Veteran's Appeals.

Business Address
U.S. Court of Veterans Appeals
625 Indiana Avenue, N.W.
Suite 900
Washington, D.C. 20004
(202) 501-5886

Senator Robert Krueger (D., Texas)

Krueger was appointed to the Senate in January 1993 to fill the vacancy created when President Clinton named Democratic Senator Lloyd Bentsen to be Secretary of the Treasury. He served for five months before he lost a special election to Republican Kay Bailey Hutchison. Krueger also served in the House from 1975 to 1979.

In 1994, Clinton named Krueger to be Ambassador to Burundi.

Representative Robert Lagomarsino (R., California)

Elected to the House in 1974, Lagomarsino was defeated in the 1992 Republican primary by Michael Huffington. The loss still bothers Lagomarsino. "I remain very upset about it, Lagomarsino told the *Los Angeles Times*. "Time doesn't change what happened."

Today, Lagomarsino is still bitter toward Huffington, who announced just eight months into his House term that he was going to challenge Democratic Senator Dianne Feinstein in 1994. Lagomarsino, who was known as a loyal Republican, gave Feinstein his opposition research files on Huffington. Lagomarsino told the *San Francisco Chronicle* that "Huffington would do our state and country and party damage."

"It was a bit of a reach for me to approach the Feinstein people, but I didn't do it because I'm supporting her," he said. "I'm opposing him. What was the point of getting rid of one congressman if the other one decides to leave?"

Lagomarsino refunded $19,889 in leftover campaign money after his defeat.

Home Address
3040 Solimar Beach Drive
Ventura, California 93001
(805) 643-5914

Representative Delbert Latta (R., Ohio)

Latta was elected to the House in 1958 and retired in 1988. He was the ranking Republican on the House Budget Committee.

Latta now lives in his old house in Bowling Green, Ohio. For the last 15 years of his House service, Latta said he kept only a small apartment in Washington.

"I'm practicing a little law," Latta said. "I help my wife out around the house. We have our granddaughter with us during the day -- her parents both work."

Latta says that he is still a "little involved" in politics and donated $47,725 in leftover campaign funds to other candidates. Latta gave the remaining $75,150 to charitable causes in Ohio, including colleges and medical institutions.

Home Address
516 Hillchrest Drive
Bowling Green, Ohio 43402
(419) 352-8627

Senator Paul Laxalt (R., Nevada)

Elected to the Senate in 1974, Laxalt retired in 1986. He formed The Laxalt Group in Washington, where he shares an office suite with former Senator Russell

Long's (D., La.) Long Law Firm.

A registered foreign agent, Laxalt's firm has represented Burlington Northern Railroad, General Pharmaceutical Industry Association, Harvey's Resort Hotel and Casino, Milliken & Company, Operaciones Turisticas (OPTUR S.A.), and Transcontinental Properties.

Business Address
The Laxalt Group
Market Square
801 Pennsylvania Avenue, N.W.
Suite 750
Washington, D.C. 20004
(202) 624-0640

Representative Marvin Leath (D., Texas)

Leath was elected to the House in 1978 and retired in 1990.

In 1993, Leath joined former Republican Representative Tom Loeffler of Texas in the lobbying firm of Loeffler & Leath, but the firm failed after just four months. He now runs Marvin Leath & Associates and has been hired by Thiokol Corporation and Fabrique Nationale Nouvelle Herstal S.A. to lobby on Defense Department authorizations and appropriations. Leath was a member of the Armed Services Committee.

Leath converted more than $42,000 in leftover campaign funds to personal use. He also donated $320,000 to the Baptist Foundation of Texas and made an unexplained $131,717 payment to the Internal Revenue Service. Leath kept a 1990 Lincoln Town Car that his campaign committee had purchased for $23,284 and reported $19,000 in post-retirement expenses.

Business Address
Marvin Leath & Associates
One Massachusetts Ave., N.W.
Suite 330
Washington, D.C. 20001
(202) 775-7100

Representative William Lehman (D., Florida)

Elected to the House in 1972, Lehman retired in 1992. He is now a lobbyist for Miami-based Blockbuster Corporation and represents the company before the Appropriations Subcommittee on Transportation, of which he was formerly a member. He is promoting a request for $42 million in federal funds to construct interchanges at Blockbuster's planned theme park in South Florida.

Lehman also is a part-time director of the Metro-Dade Transit Agency.

Lehman converted approximately $20,000 in leftover campaign funds to personal use, including bills for a personal trainer and pool service. He also gave his nine-year-old grandson a $1,000 check, saying that it was an early contribution to a congressional campaign in 2012.

Business Address
Metro-Dade Transit Agency
33309 North West 23nd Avenue
Miami, Florida 33142
(305) 637-3814

Home Address
711 North East 118th Street
Biscayne Park, Florida 33161

Representative Mickey Leland (D. Texas)

Leland, who was elected to the House in 1978, was killed in a plane crash in Africa while on a congressional trip in 1989.

Representative Norman Lent (R., New York)

Lent was elected to the House in 1970 and retired in 1992.

He is now a partner with Michael Scrivner, his former congressional chief of staff, in the lobbying firm of Lent & Scrivner. The firm's clients have included Makowski Associates, Inc., MFJ Task Force (a coalition of regional Bell operating companies), Mobil Oil Corporation and Pfizer Corporation.

In addition to transferring $570,000 of leftover campaign funds to the Lent Family Charitable Trust, Lent contributed more than $18,000 in leftover campaign funds to former House colleagues, including $2,000 to Representative John Dingell (D., Mich), then-chair of the Energy and Commerce Committee.

Business Address
Lent & Scrivner
1300 I. Street, N.W.
Suite 250 W
Washington, D.C. 20005
(202) 789-4161

Home Address
2336 South Queen Street
Arlington, Virginia 22202
(703) 892-8390

Representative Mel Levine (D., California)

Elected to the House in 1982, Levine gave up his seat in 1992 to make an unsuccessful run for the Senate. He is now a partner in the Los Angeles law firm of Gibson, Dunn & Crutcher, which is a registered foreign agent and lobbying firm.

The firm's clients have included Chase Manhattan Bank, Genentech, Inc., the Kuwait-American Foundation, the National Knitwear and Sportswear Association, Teamwork America, and the UNOCAL Corporation.

Business Address
Gibson, Dunn & Crutcher
2029 Century Park East
41st Floor
Los Angeles, California 90067
(310) 552-8574

Representative Elliott Levitas (D., Georgia)

Levitas was elected to the House in 1974 and served until he was defeated in 1984 by Pat Swindall. Today, he is a practicing attorney with the law firm of Kilpatrick & Cody. "I divide my time between the Atlanta office of Kilpatrick & Cody and the Washington office, with the majority of my time being in Atlanta," Levitas says. "My areas of activity include litigation, federal and state government procurement management and litigation, environmental law, federal and state administrative law and regulatory practice, and strategic management of federal and state government relations."

Levitas represents an office development in Southwest Washington, The Portals, which is suing the federal government over the cancellation of a lease that would have moved the Federal Communications Commission to The Portals.

"If they can use a scam of this sort to undo a procurement that has cost millions of dollars, taken five years, and for legitimate reason [cancel it], then there is no reason to put any credibility in the government's procurement process," Levitas told *National Journal* in May 1994. The case is now in appeal.

Business Address
Kilpatrick & Cody
1100 Peachtree Street
Suite 2800
Atlanta, Georgia 30309
(404) 815-6500
and Kilpatrick & Cody
700 13th Street, N.W.
Suite 800
Washington, D.C. 20005
(202) 508-5815

Home Address
829 Castle Falls Drive, N.E.
Atlanta, Georgia 30329
(404) 636-9803

Representative Tom Loeffler (R., Texas)

Elected to the House in 1978, Loeffler gave up his seat in 1986 for an unsuccessful gubernatorial bid. In 1987, President Reagan named him the principal coordinator for Central America in the White House's Office of Legislative Affairs.

Since then, Loeffler has been a Washington lobbyist with various firms, including a short stint with former Democratic Representative Marvin Leath of Texas. Loeffler is now working as a lawyer and lobbyist in the Washington office of Arter & Hadden, a Cleveland-based firm, with former Democratic Representative Dennis Eckart of Ohio.

In Texas, Loeffler is also working to attract the 1996 Republican National Convention to San Antonio. "When you're looking at the political dynamics of 1996, the South is extremely fertile ground for the Republican Party," Loeffler told the *Houston Chronicle*.

Business Address
Arter & Hadden
1800 K Street, N.W., Suite 400K
Washington, D.C. 20006
(202) 775-7100
and Arter & Hadden, Johnson & Bromberg
1717 Main Street, Suite 410
Dallas, Texas 75201-4605
(214) 761-2100 and

Business Address, cont'd.
Arter & Hadden
7710 Jones Maltsberger
Suite 540
San Antonio, Texas 78216
(210) 805-8497

Representative Cathy Long (D., Louisiana)

Long was elected to the House in March 1985 to fill the seat left vacant by the death of her husband, Gillis Long, in January 1985. She retired after one term. Long spent $448,663 of her husband's leftover campaign money to finance her congressional race.

Home Address
2500 Virginia Avenue, N.W.
Washington, D.C. 20037
(202) 625-2895

Representative Clarence Long (D., Maryland)

Long was elected to the House in 1962 and served until 1984, when he was unseated by Republican Helen Delich Bentley. He died on September 19, 1994, at age 85.

Representative Gillis Long (D., Louisiana)

Elected to the House in 1963, Long died in office on January 20, 1985. His wife, Cathy Long, converted his $448,663 in leftover campaign funds for use in her campaign to succeed him.

Senator Russell Long (D., Louisiana)

Long was elected to the Senate in 1948 and retired in 1986. He now runs the Long Law Firm in Baton Rouge and Washington and is a registered lobbyist. Long shares the Washington office with The Laxalt Group, the firm of former Republican Senator Paul Laxalt.

Business Address
Long Law Firm
Market Square
801 Pennsylvania Avenue, N.W.
Suite 750
Washington, D.C. 20004
(202) 737-9212

Representative Trent Lott (R., Mississippi)

Lott was elected to the House in 1972 and to the Senate, where he currently serves, in 1988. He was reelected in 1994.

Business Address
487 Russell Senate Office Building
Washington, D.C. 20510
(202) 224-6253

Representative Mike Lowry (D., Washington)

Elected to the House in 1978, he gave up his seat in 1988 to make an unsuccessful bid for the Senate. In 1992 he was elected governor of Washington.

Business Address
Office of the Governor
P.O. Box 40002
Olympia, Washington 98504
(206) 753-6780

Representative Bill Lowery (R., California)

Lowery was elected to the House in 1980 and retired in 1992 after it was disclosed that he had 300 overdrafts at the House bank. He is now a partner in the Washington lobbying firm of Copeland, Hatfield, Lowery and Jacquez. In 1992, Lowery told the *Los Angeles Times* that Congress had begun to lose its appeal to him. "It has not been satisfying," he said. "Since 1989, Congress has not been able to get past the gridlock and partisan bickering."

"Though I'm not in Congress anymore, I continue to serve Californians," Lowery says. "In my current position as partner with the firm of Copeland, Hatfield, Lowery and Jacquez, I do a lot of work with defense conversion, dual use, and base reuse, which are important issues for residents of my home state. The firm also handles issues related to the environment, transportation, health care, and a variety of others. Our clients come from all over California, and include the State of California, Alameda and Merced Counties, Bay Area Rapid Transit, Pacific Mutual, San Diego State University Foundation, Southwest Marine, Science Applications International Corporation, Monarch Wines, and more. I'm very happy with what I'm doing and proud to be working with such a good group of people."

Lowery refunded $35,795 in leftover campaign contributions.

Business Address
Copeland, Hatfield, Lowery & Jacquez
607 13th Street, N.W.
#710 North
Washington, D.C. 20005
(202) 347-5990

Representative Manuel Lujan (R., New Mexico)

Elected to the House in 1968, Lujan served until 1989 when he became Secretary of the Interior in the Bush Administration. He is now a consultant in Albuquerque, New Mexico. Lujan is a director of Sodak Gaming, Inc., which distributes gaming equipment and finances Indian gaming enterprises.

According to congressional testimony in July 1994, by Sodak's vice president, Knute Knudson, Jr., more than 95 percent of Sodak's business is with Indian tribes.

In his testimony, Knudson complained about extensive governmental regulation of Indian gaming. "Manuel Lujan, who is a member of the board of directors of Sodak Gaming, Inc., has indicated that he received stricter scrutiny and more background checks as a member of our board of directors than he received to become Secretary of the Interior'."

Business Address
Manuel Lujan Associates
P.O. Box 3727
Albuquerque, New Mexico 87190
(505)266-7771

Representative Charles Luken (D., Ohio)

Luken was elected to the House in 1990 to succeed his father, Representative Thomas Luken. At age 40, Luken surprised his constituents when he announced that he was retiring from the House after just one term. Luken faced no Republican opposition and had just won the Democratic primary when he made the announcement.

"I miss my wife and children when I'm away, and it has been harder on me than I expected," Luken said in his announcement. "I've never felt it's [the House] been a productive experience."

Luken was mayor of Cincinnati when his father retired after 14 years in the House. "Charlie didn't like what he was doing, so he got out," Thomas Luken told reporters. He is now a television anchorman with WLWT-TV/Channel 5 in Cincinnati.

He gave $55,950 in leftover campaign funds to other political campaigns and donated $110,000 to the Ohio State Treasury to help pay for the special primary election to select his replacement.

Business Address
WLWT-TV/Channel 5
140 West 9th Street
Cincinnati, Ohio 45202
(513) 353-5011

Representative Thomas Luken (D., Ohio)

Elected to the House in 1976, Luken retired in 1990 and was succeeded by Charles Luken, his son. After Congress, Luken joined the Washington law firm of Reed, Smith, Shawy & McClay as a lobbyist.

In November 1993, Luken was elected to the Cincinnati City Council. Luken had served on the city council and as mayor before his election to Congress. He has left Reed, Smith and works full-time on the council.

Business Address
Cincinnati City Council
801 Plum Street
Room 308, City Hall
Cincinnati, Ohio 45202
(513) 352-3346

Home Address
5300 Hamilton Avenue
Cincinnati, Ohio 45224
(513) 541-1322

Representative Donald E. "Buz" Lukens (R., Ohio)

Elected to the House in 1966, Lukens gave up his seat in 1970 to make an unsuccessful run for governor. In 1971, he was elected to the Ohio State Senate where he served until he was again elected to Congress in 1986. Lukens was forced to resign from the House in October 1990 after he was convicted of charges that he had sex with a 16-year-old girl and then offered her mother a government job to silence her. He lives in Washington.

Representative Stan Lundine (D., New York)

Elected to the House in a special election on March 6, 1976, Lundine left when he was elected lieutenant governor of New York. He ran for his third consecutive term in 1994 but was defeated. Mail will be forwarded to his current business address.

Business Address
Lieutenant Governor's Office
State Capitol Room 247
Albany, New York 12224
(518) 473-2061

Representative Daniel Lungren (R., California)

Elected to the House in 1978, Lungren left in 1988 when he was appointed state treasurer of California. When his appointment was rejected by the state senate, however, Lungren returned to private law practice. He was elected attorney general of California in 1990 and reelected in 1994.

"Sometimes defeat requires you to look inside and see what you've done wrong. We have tasted defeat and it's sour, and we don't want to do that again," Lungren said of Republicans in June 1993.

Lungren used $16,170 in leftover campaign funds to reimburse himself for moving expenses.

Business Address
State of California
1515 K Street, Suite 600
Sacramento, California 95814
(916) 324-5437

Representative Buddy MacKay (D., Florida)

Elected to the House in 1982, MacKay gave up his seat in 1988 to make an unsuccessful bid for the Senate. He was elected lieutenant governor of Florida in 1990 and reelected in 1994.

Business Address
The Capitol, Room PL05
Tallahassee, Florida 32399
(904) 488-4711

Representative Edward Madigan (R., Illinois)

Madigan was elected to the House in 1972 and served until President Bush named him Secretary of Agriculture in 1991. In 1993, Madigan briefly joined the Washington lobbying firm of McLeod, Watkinson & Miller.

Madigan then worked in Washington as a lobbyist for State Farm Insurance Company. In July 1994, he made a controversial move when he endorsed Democratic Senator Bob Kerrey of Nebraska over his Republican opponent. "I cannot stress strongly enough to my Republican friends and to my farm and ranch friends in Nebraska the importance of Bob Kerrey's reelection to the future of agriculture in Nebraska," Madigan said at the time.

Madigan converted $25,000 in leftover campaign funds to personal use. He used another $433,591 to establish a personal trust, which he said is managed by an unnamed charity, and spent $54,280 in post-retirement employee fees and expenses.

Madigan died on December 7, 1994, at age 58.

Representative Ron Marlenee (R., Montana)

Elected to the House in 1976, Marlenee lost the 1992 election to Democratic Representative Pat Williams after Montana lost one of its two congressional seats as a result of reapportionment.

Marlenee has remained in Washington and works as a lobbyist on "sportsman issues."

Business Address
Capital Consulting
8626 Lee Highway
Fairfax, Virginia 22031
(703) 876-0400

Representative Dan Marriott (R. Utah)

Marriott, who was elected to the House in 1976, gave up his seat in 1984 to make an unsuccessful gubernatorial bid. He is still active in politics, and the *Salt Lake City Tribune* recently called him "a rebel on the horizon." Marriott now runs Dan Marriott and Company, which is involved in restaurant management and insurance.

Business Address
Dan Marriott & Company
57 West South Temple
Suite 200
Salt Lake City, Utah 84101
(801) 363-1000

Home Address
2024 Princeton Drive
Salt Lake City, Utah 84108
(801) 581-1937

Representative David Martin (R., New York)

Martin was elected to the House in 1980 and retired in 1992. After his retirement, Martin actually worked for a few months in the congressional office of his successor, John McHugh. Martin is now the vice president for state and local affairs of the National Soft Drink Association.

Business Address
National Soft Drink Association
1101 16th Street, N.W.
Washington, D.C. 20036
(202) 463-6732

Representative James Martin (R., North Carolina)

Elected to the House in 1972, Martin served six terms until he was elected governor of North Carolina in 1984. He is now the chairman of the Research Development Board of the Carolinas Medical Center in Charlotte, North Carolina.

Business Address
Carolinas Medical Center
P.O. Box 32861
Charlotte, North Carolina 28232
(704) 355-3959

Home Address
1831 Maryland Avenue
Charlotte, North Carolina 28209
(704) 335-1422

Representative Lynn Martin (R., Illinois)

Elected to the House in 1980, Martin gave up her seat in 1990 to unsuccessfully challenge Democratic Senator Paul Simon. President Bush named her Secretary of Labor in 1991.

Martin later taught a course at Harvard University's John F. Kennedy School of Government. Now living in Chicago, she is a director of several corporations, including Ameritech, the Chicago Zoo, and Deloitte & Touche. Martin is also an adviser to Deloitte & Touche and also holds the Davee Chair at Northwestern University's J.L. Kellogg School of Management.

"If the presidency had remained in control of one party for almost 30 years, that fact -- and its implications for our political and governmental system -- would be the topic of half of the newspaper columns and Ph.D. theses in political science," she said when she was in the House. The Democrats have been in control of the House of Representatives for that long -- and no one seems to notice."

Martin used approximately $15,800 in leftover campaign funds to pay for post-retirement expenses.

Business Address
180 North Stetson Avenue
Suite 200
Chicago, Illinois 60601-6779
(312) 946-3000
and J.L. Kellogg School of Management
Northwestern University
2001 Sheridan Road
Evanston, Illinois 60208

Senator Mack Mattingly (R., Georgia)

Elected to the Senate in 1980, Mattingly was unseated by Democrat Wyche Fowler in 1986.

In 1987 President Reagan named him Assistant Secretary General for Defense Support, NATO, in Brussels, and in 1989 President Bush named him Ambassador to Seychelles. In a 1993 interview, Mattingly told a reporter that his responsibilities as ambassador included protecting an Air Force satellite tracking station making sure "that everything stays on an even keel." He lives in Georgia.

Senator Spark Matsunaga (D., Hawaii)

Matsunaga was elected to the House in 1962 and to the Senate in 1976. He died in office in April 1990.

Senator Charles Mathias (R., Maryland)

Mathias was elected to the House in 1961 and to the Senate in 1968, from which he retired in 1986. After his retirement, Mathias worked as a partner in the Washington office of the law firm of Jones, Day, Reavis & Pogue.

Named chairman of First American Bankshares in January 1993, Mathias also works with an organization that opposes the use of filibusters in the Senate.

"When I came to the Senate in 1969, a filibuster was a major event," he wrote in an op-ed piece for *The Washington Post* in June 1994. "In order to prevent a majority from voting to pass a bill, determined opponents would refuse to end debate. Their strategy was to bring all Senate action to a halt until the Senate gave up its attempt to pass the legislation. Today, filibusters are far less visible but far more frequent. The filibuster has become an epidemic, used whenever a coalition can find 41 voted to oppose legislation. The distinction between voting against legislation and blocking a vote, between opposing and obstructing, has nearly disappeared."

Business Address	*Home Address*
First American Bankshares	3808 Leland Street
740 15th Street, N.W.	Chevy Chase, Maryland 20815
8th Floor	
Washington, D.C. 20005	
(202) 383-1404	

Representative Nicholas Mavroules (D., Massachusetts)

Elected to the House in 1978, Mavroules was unseated in 1992 by Republican Peter Torkildsen. In April 1993, Mavroules pleaded guilty to 15 counts of racketeering and extortion for accepting illegal gratuities and failing to report income. He was released in July 1994 from the McKean County Federal Correctional Institute in Bradford, Pennsylvania, after serving a 15-month sentence.

He could not be located.

Senator James McClure (R., Idaho)

McClure was elected to the House in 1966 and to the Senate in 1972. He retired in 1990. After his retirement, McClure opened a Washington lobbying firm, McClure, Gerard & Neuenschwander, that represents many of the nation's largest mining companies. McClure is a former chairman of the Senate Natural Resources Committee. Jack Gerard and Tod Neuenschwander are both former congressional aides to McClure. McClure also is of counsel to the Idaho law firm of Givens, Pursley & Huntley.

See chapter "The Revolving Door."

Business Address
McClure, Gerard & Neuenschwander
801 Pennsylvania Avenue, N.W.
Suite 820
Washington, D.C. 20004
(202) 393-0545
and Given, Pursley & Huntly
277 North 6th Street, Suite 200
Park Place
P.O. Box 2720
Boise, Idaho 83701

Home Address
9440 West Pebblebrook Lane
Boise, Idaho 83703

Representative Bob McEwen (R., Ohio)

Elected to the House in 1980, McEwen was unseated in 1992 by Democrat Ted Strickland after it was disclosed that he had 166 overdrafts at the House bank. A few months after he lost that race, McEwen ran for the House again in a special election to fill the vacancy created by the resignation of Representative Bill Gradison, but he lost the Republican primary.

He now runs McEwen Enterprises and is associated with the Washington lobbying firm of Morgan, Casener Associates, Inc.

Business Address
Morgan, Casener Associates
1332 Independence Avenue, S.E.
Washington, D.C. 20003
(202) 543-4600
and McEwen Enterprises
(703) 354-7454

Home Address
7528 Royce Court
Annandale, Virginia 22003
(703) 354-1071

Representative Raymond McGrath (R., New York)

Elected to the House in 1980, McGrath retired in 1992 to become the president of the Washington-based Beer Institute. A former member of the Ways and Means Committee, McGrath now lobbies his old colleagues on proposed alcohol taxes.

Business Address
The Beer Institute
1225 I Street, N.W.
Suite 825
Washington, D.C. 20005
(202) 737-2377

Representative Matthew McHugh (D., New York)

McHugh was elected to the House in 1974 and retired in 1992. He served for a short time as the vice president of Cornell University and then returned to Washington as the counselor to the president of the World Bank.

McHugh gave more than $75,000 in leftover campaign funds to political and charitable organizations.

Business Address
World Bank
1818 H Street, N.W.
Washington, D.C. 20433
(202) 458-0309

Home Address
2420 Lancaster Court
Falls Church, Virginia

Representative Stewart McKinney (R., Connecticut)

Elected to the House in 1970, McKinney died in office on May 7, 1987.

Representative John McKernan (R., Maine)

McKernan, who was elected to the House in 1982, served until 1986, when he was elected governor of Maine. He served his last year as governor in 1994 and is prohibited from running for a third consecutive term. McKernan is married to Republican Representative Olympia Snowe of Maine, who was elected to the Senate in 1994. His current address is not available.

Representative Tom McMillen (D., Maryland)

McMillen, who was elected to the House in 1986, lost the 1992 election to Republican Representative Wayne Gilchrest after redistricting combined their districts.

McMillen is now the chairman and president of CliniCorp Northeast Division, a subsidiary of Clinicorp, Inc., which owns and manages chiropractic clinics.

President Clinton appointed McMillen, a Rhodes scholar and former National Basketball Association player, to co-chair the President's Council on Physical Fitness. "Little League waiting lines are sometimes a mile long," McMillen told the Associated Press in June 1994. "You go to a school and you see the lack of opportunities there, the lack of community programs. Not only are we not educating kids in healthy lifestyles, but we're not giving them an opportunity to recreate."

Business Address
CliniCorp
1601 Belvedere Road
Suite 500E
West Palm Beach, Florida 33406
(407) 684-2225

Home Address
1103 South Carolina Avenue, S.E.
Washington, D.C. 20003
(202) 544-1085

Representative James McNulty (D., Arizona)

Elected to the House in 1982, McNulty was unseated in 1984 by Jim Kolbe. He now works as a lawyer in Tucson, Arizona.

Business Address
1 South Church Avenue
Tucson, Arizona 85701
(602) 798-7900

Senator John Melcher (D., Montana)

Melcher was elected to the House in a special election in June 1969 and was elected to the Senate in 1976. He lost his Senate seat in 1988 to Republican Conrad Burns.

Melcher attempted a comeback in 1994 but lost the Democratic primary. His campaign television ads portrayed him as still in office. "An effective fighter for Montanans, John Melcher believes we need to get back to work in the U.S. Senate for Montana," an announcer said in one commercial. "He works hard for agriculture, for small business and working people everywhere . . . Montana's John Melcher."

However, Melcher has lived and worked in Washington since his 1988 loss, however, and is a registered foreign agent. His clients have included the Philippine Coconut Authority and the Seaweed Industry Association of the Philippines. A veterinarian by profession, Melcher has also represented the American Veterinarian Medical Association before the Food and Drug Administration.

Melcher said that he spends about a fourth of his time in Washington donating time and money as a board member of CARE, a not-for-profit, humanitarian relief organization. "I help them in any way possible," he said.

Business Address
230-B Maryland Avenue, N.E.
Washington, D.C. 20002
(202) 546-4084

Home Address
12308 Arrow Park Drive
Fort Washington, Maryland 20744
(301) 292-4664

Representative Dan Mica (D., Florida)

Mica, who was elected to the House in 1978, gave up his seat in 1988 to make an unsuccessful bid for the Senate. He lost the Democratic primary to fellow Representative Buddy MacKay.

Today, Mica is the executive vice president for Federal Affairs of the American Council of Life Insurance (ACLI). In May 1994, he testified before the Senate Commerce, Science and Transportation Committee on assumption reinsurance.

President Clinton named Mica the chairman of the Board of International Broadcasting, on which he has served since 1991.

Business Address	*Home Address*
American Council of Life Insurance	7307 Burtonwood Drive
1001 Pennsylvania Avenue, N.W.	Alexandria, Virginia 22307
Washington, D.C. 20004	(703) 660-9241
(202) 624-2121	

Representative Clarence Miller (R., Ohio)

Elected to the House in 1966, Miller lost the 1992 Republican primary to fellow Representative Bob McEwen, after redistricting combined their districts. Miller, now retired, lives in Arlington, Virginia.

Home Address
1655 B. South Hayes Street
Arlington, Virginia 22202
(703) 521-5613

Representative John Miller (R., Washington)

Elected to the House in 1984, Miller retired in 1992. He has returned to Seattle where he works for the investment banking firm of Chaner, Painter Company, Ltd. Miller is also associated with Seattle's Discovery Institute.

Business Address	*Home Address*
Chaner, Painter Company, Ltd.	10643 Culpepper Court, N.W.
Columbia Center	Seattle, Washington 98177
701 5th Avenue	(206) 362-5863
Suite 7150	
Seattle, Washington 98104	
(206) 386-5656	

Representative Joseph Minish (D., New Jersey)

Minish, who was elected to the House in 1962, was unseated in 1984 by Dean Gallo. Today, he is a business consultant in New Jersey.

Home Address
66 Sheridan Avenue
West Orange, New Jersey 07052
(201) 731-6789

Representative Parren Mitchell (D., Maryland),

Mitchell, who was elected to the House in 1970, gave up his seat in 1986 to make an unsuccessful run for lieutenant governor of Maryland.

As the founder and chairman of the Minority Business Enterprise Legal Defense and Education Fund, a not-for-profit public-interest law firm, Mitchell has remained active in issues that affect minority-owned small businesses. He was the chairman of the House Small Business Committee.

Business Address
Minority Business Enterprise
220 I Street, N.E.
Suite 280
Washington, D.C. 20002
(202) 543-0040

Representative Guy Molinari (R., New York)

Molinari, who was elected to the House in 1980, resigned in November 1989 after he was elected Staten Island Borough President. He was succeeded in the House by Susan Molinari, his daughter.

In July 1994, Susan Molinari married fellow Representative Bill Paxon. "This is every politician's dream, to have a daughter who's a star and to have a son-in-law who's equally a star," Molinari told *Roll Call*.

"Throughout my years in public service, I have been fortunate to have the opportunity to serve at all three levels of government," Molinari says in his official biography. "It has given me a unique perspective into my present office as Borough President of Staten Island. Politics seems to run in my family, as my father S. Robert Molinari became the first Italian immigrant to serve in the New York State Legislature, and my daughter, Susan Molinari, served as Minority Leader in the City Council before succeeding me in Congress. While I have represented

Staten Island as a State Assemblyman and U.S. Congressman, my present post as Borough President has brought me closest to the issues and problems affecting my home borough."

Business Address
Borough of Staten Island
Borough Hall
Staten Island, New York 10301
(718) 816-1049

Representative David Monson (R., Utah)

Elected to the House in 1984, Monson served one term before he retired in 1986. He could not be located.

Representative Jim Moody (D., Wisconsin)

Moody, who was elected to the House in 1982, gave up his seat in 1992 to make an unsuccessful bid for the Senate. He holds a doctorate in economics, and after he left Congress joined the Medical College of Wisconsin's Health Policy Institute as a visiting professor. Moody also became a vice president of Chambers Associates, a Washington lobbying firm that has a number of health care clients.

So, when Moody testified before the House Ways and Means Subcommittee on Health in February 1994, he was not only a Wisconsin professor, as he described himself, but also a Washington lobbyist.

"The Clinton blueprint promises to fundamentally alter the coverage, cost and fairness of the American health system," Moody told members of the subcommittee. "But beneath the surface of glossy averages, there are pockets of disadvantaged population in our country, especially in our inner cities, which will need targeted resources beyond those created by market forces of managed competition and some policy adjustments to the proposed legislation, if these disadvantaged groups are to share in the promise of dramatic improvement."

Chambers Associates has represented the American Hospital Association, the American Postal Workers Union, Blue Cross of Western Pennsylvania, Belk Store Services, the Edison Electric Institute, the Greater New York Hospital Association, Marriott Corporation, the National Committee to Preserve Social Security and Medicare, the National Council of Chain Restaurants, U.S. West, U.S.X. Corporation, and Walter Industries.

Business Address   *Home Address*
Chambers Associates   4326 Wildwood Avenue
1625 K Street, N.W, Suite 200   Shorewood, Wisconsin 53211
Washington, D.C. 20006   (414) 962-2847

and Medical College of Wisconsin
8701 Watertown Plank Road
Milwaukee, Wisconsin 53226
(414) 257-8762

Representative Bruce Morrison (D., Connecticut)

Elected to the House in 1982, Morrison served until 1990 when he gave up his seat in 1990 to make an unsuccessful run for the governor's office. He now practices law in New Haven, Connecticut.

Business Address
2 Whitney Avenue, Suite 700
New Haven, Connecticut 06510
(203) 498-0086

Representative Sid Morrison (R., Washington)

Elected to the House in 1980, Morrison gave up his seat in 1992 to make an unsuccessful gubernatorial bid. He now works for the winner of the governor's race, Mike Lowry, as the state's Secretary of Transportation.

Business Address
Washington State Department of Transportation
P.O. Box 47316
Olympia, Washington 98504
(206) 705-7054

Representative Robert Mrazek (D., New York)

Elected to the House in 1982, Mrazek retired in 1992 after it was disclosed that he had 920 overdrafts at the House bank. In January 1993, Mrazek had a benign tumor removed from the base of his skull.

Home Address
301 Constitution Avenue, N.E.
Washington, D.C. 20002

Representative David Nagle (D., Iowa)

Elected to the House in 1986, Nagle was unseated in 1992 by Republican Jim Nussle. In 1994, Nagle ran against Nussle in an attempt to regain his House seat, but lost.

but lost.

"I'm almost ready to start a congressional sabbatical program," Nagle told *Roll Call*. "[Members of Congress] live in metal tubes -- that's just the nature of the job. It's incredible how much more of the community you absorb when you live in it every day."

"We took a psychiatric exam, and we failed it," Nagle joked. "So we're going to run."

Business Address
David Nagle Law Office
4935 North Union Road
Cedar Falls, Iowa 50613
(319) 234-3623

Representative Bill Nelson (D., Florida)

Elected to the House in 1978, Nelson gave up his seat in 1990 to make an unsuccessful gubernatorial bid. A highlight of his congressional career was his flight on the space shuttle in January, 1986. Nelson practiced law in Melbourne, Florida, where he developed a space law section for his firm.

In 1994, Nelson ran for Insurance Commissioner of Florida and won. "I am what I am," Nelson told the *Orlando Sentinel*. "After almost two decades of service, I was voluntarily retired three-and-a-half years ago. I'm ready for public service again."

Business Address   *Home Address*
Department of Insurance   3000 Rock Point Road
Capital Plaza, Level 11   Melbourne, Florida 32950
Tallahassee, Florida 32399   (407) 723-6802
(904) 413-1776

Representative Howard Neilson (R., Utah)

Neilson, who was elected to the House in 1982, retired in 1990.

"I announced my retirement in December 1989, in the middle of my fourth term," Neilson said. "I had won election easily -- from 67 percent to 78 percent -- and could likely have stayed in Congress much longer. Many questioned my decision just as a large raise and significantly higher pension were in the offing, but monetary considerations were never part of my decision to run in the first place or to remain in office."

"We left Congress to serve as full-time missionaries for the Church of Jesus Christ of Latter-Day Saints (Mormon). As you know, we pay all of our own ex-

sion as a youth because I was in the service in World War II. My wife and I wanted to serve while we had the health and energy required."

". . . I came to the conclusion that the vast majority of the representatives do their very best to represent those who sent them. They were and are a very conscientious group with whom I was proud to associate."

Home Address
580 Sagewood Avenue
Provo, Utah 84604

Representative Bill Nichols (D., Alabama)

Elected to the House in 1966, Nichols died in office on December 13, 1988.

Representative Dick Nichols (R., Kansas)

Nichols, who was elected to the House in 1990, served one term before he lost to Eric Yost in the 1992 Republican primary. He returned to his former job as Chairman of the Board of Home State Bank & Trust in McPherson, Kansas.

Business Address
Home State Bank & Trust
P.O. Box 1266
McPherson, Kansas 67460
(316) 241-3732

Home Address
404 Lakeside Drive
McPherson, Kansas 67460

Representative Henry Nowak (D., New York)

Nowak, who was elected to the House in 1974, retired in 1992. He now works as a consultant for Marine Midland Bank in Buffalo, New York.

Nowak contributed more than $110,000 of leftover campaign funds to political and other charitable causes.

Business Address
Marine Midland Bank
1 Marine Midland Center
Buffalo, New York 14203
(716) 833-6333

Home Address
40 Agassiz Circle
Buffalo, New York 14214
(716) 881-2129

Representative George O'Brien (D., Illinois)

O'Brien, who was elected to the House in 1972, died in office on July 17, 1986. His widow received $65,355 in leftover campaign funds.

Representative Mary Rose Oakar (D., Ohio)

Elected to the House in 1976, Oakar lost the 1992 election after she had 213 overdrafts at the House bank. Oakar has returned to Cleveland where she is the president of Oakar & Associates, a lobbying and public relations firm.

In June 1994, Oakar's congressional personnel and salary records were subpoenaed by Justice Department investigators in connection with the House bank probe. Oakar's former executive assistant, Janice A. Papez, testified before a federal grand jury on June 29, 1994, about Oakar's involvement with the bank.

President Clinton appointed Oakar to the White House Conference on Aging on July 22, 1994.

Business Address
Oakar & Associates
2621 Lorain Avenue
Cleveland, Ohio 44113
(216) 522-0550

Representative Jim Olin (D., Virginia)

Olin was elected to the House in 1982 and retired in 1992. Olin was the treasurer of the Garth Newl Music Center in Warm Springs, Virginia until June 1994. Today, he is working as a volunteer with the Concord Coalition and says that he "hopes to have some influence on getting the federal budget deficit down to close to zero by the year 2000."

Home Address
175 27th Street, S.E.
Roanoke, Virginia 24014
(703) 345-1114

Representative Thomas P. "Tip" O'Neill (D., Massachusetts)

Elected to the house in 1952, O'Neill became speaker in 1977. He retired in 1986 and died on January 5, 1994.

Representative Richard Ottinger (D., New York)

Ottinger, who co-founded the Peace Corps in 1961, was elected to the House in 1964. He gave up his seat in 1970 to make an unsuccessful bid for the Senate, and in 1972 lost a congressional race. In 1974, Ottinger was finally reelected to the

Today, Ottinger is a professor of law at Pace University Law School and says that he is not active in politics aside from his membership on the boards of Renew America and the Energy Study Institute. He also served on former New York Governor Mario Cuomo's Environmental Advisory Board. "I help the local candidates but other than that, not much," he said.

Business Address	*Home Address*
Pace University Law School	818 The Cresent
78 North Broadway	Mamaroneck, New York 10543
White Plains, N.Y. 10603	
(914) 422-4324	

Representative Wayne Owens (D., Utah)

Elected to the House in 1972, Owens gave up his seat after one term to mount an unsuccessful Senate campaign. He was reelected to the House in 1986 and retired in 1992.

Owens is now a lawyer in the Washington office of Weil, Gotshal & Manges, a New York-based firm. The firm's clients have included the government of Jordan and the American Association of Meat Processors.

Business Address
Weil, Gotshal & Manges
1615 L Street, N.W.
Suite 700
Washington, D.C. 20036
(202) 682-7000

Representative Leon Panetta (D., California)

Panetta, who was elected to the House in 1976, left in 1993 to become the director of the Office of Management and Budget in the Clinton Administration. Panetta was named White House Chief of Staff in June 1994.

Business Address
The White House
1600 Pennsylvania Avenue, N.W.
Washington, D.C. 20500
(202) 456-6797

Representative Stanford Parris (R., Virginia)

Elected to the House in 1972, Parris was defeated in 1974 by Herb Harris. He was again elected to the House in 1980 and served until he was unseated by Democrat James Moran in 1990. In 1989, Parris finished third in the Virginia GOP gubernatorial primary.

Parris was appointed by President Bush to a seven-year term as the administrator of the St. Lawrence Seaway Development Corporation in January 1991. The Seaway Corporation operates under the Department of Transportation and works with the Canadian government to manage a series of locks and vessel traffic on the St. Lawrence River.

Parris transferred approximately $37,000 in leftover campaign funds to a state political action committee.

Business Address
St. Lawrence Seaway Development Corporation
P.O. Box 44090
Washington, D.C. 20026
(202) 366-0118

Representative Charles Pashayan (R., California)

Pashayan was elected to the House in 1978 and served until he was unseated in 1990 by Democrat Calvin Dooley. His political trouble began when he accepted $26,000 in campaign contributions from savings-and-loan executive Charles Keating and then sought to loosen restrictions on S&Ls. He later returned the $26,000.

Home Address
748 East Holland Avenue
Fresno, California 93704
(202) 337-4343

Representative Liz Patterson (D., South Carolina)

Patterson, who was elected to the House in 1986, was unseated in 1992 by Republican Bob Inglis. In 1994, she unsuccessfully ran for lieutenant governor of South Carolina.

"Since leaving Congress in January of 1993, I have been extremely active in the community and was encouraged to seek the Democratic nomination for lieutenant governor," Patterson says. "At a time when politicians are being painted as evil, I believe it is important that we emphasize the role of public servant. Throughout my career, on city council, in the state senate, and in Congress, I worked hard to provide good constituent services. Whether I am elected lieutenant governor or not, I will continue to be active in my community."

Home Address
1275 Partridge Road
Spartanburg, South Carolina 29302
(803) 582-1970

Representative Bill Patman (D., Texas)

Elected to the House in 1980, Patman was unseated in 1984 by Republican Mac Sweeney. He now practices law in Austin, Texas.

Business Address
Meridan Executive Plaza
1601 Rio Grande Street, Suite 450
Austin, Texas 78701
(512) 474-2120

Representative Jerry Patterson (D., California)

Elected to the House in 1974, Patterson was unseated in 1984 by Republican Robert Dornan, who called him "a sneaky little dirtbag" during the campaign.

Patterson returned to California and worked as the city manager of Cypress and Lake Forest. He was fired from the Cypress job in November 1992 for allegedly giving bad legal advice to members of the city council. As a result, he also resigned from the Lake Forest position.

Today, he works as a lawyer for the firm of Burke, Williams & Sorensen.

Business Address
Burke, Williams & Sorensen
3200 Bristol Street
Suite 640
Costa Mesa, California 92648
(714) 545-5559

Home Address
501 20th Street
Huntington Beach, California 92648
(714) 969-2222

Representative Ron Paul (R., Texas)

Paul, who was elected to the House in 1976, gave up his seat to make an unsuccessful bid for the Senate in 1984. In 1988, he was the Libertarian Party's presidential nominee.

Today, Paul has returned to his profession as a practicing Obstetrician/ Gynecologist in Lake Jackson, Texas.

"When I left Congress, I went back to practicing medicine," Paul said. "I also started a business hard-money newsletter." He runs the Foundation for Rational Economics in Education (FREE) and the National Endowment for Liberty.

Paul says that leaving the House produced a "feeling of relief, a weight off my shoulders. Congress was a system that I had to respond to. It was exasperating. I didn't feel like I was losing any benefits when I left."

Term limits appeal to Paul but today, he questions them. "I had a bill in the House that limited everybody to eight years, including federal judges," he says. "But amendments are missing the point. Americans should question the role of government. Although I supported term limitations, it is treating a symptom. Ultimately, we can change the country through education. The solution has got to be what the people want from their government. We have to change people's minds."

Whenever he "toys" with the idea of running for Congress again, Paul says, he "flips on C-SPAN." He is not optimistic about the nation's economic future. "True bankruptcy of the country will happen before the end of the decade," he says. "Health care reform is just another example of the people expecting more from the government. Government created the mess, it's just going to make it worse. How long is it going to take us to come to our senses?"

Paul's wife, Carol, said that they would be on "easy street" today if Paul had not gone into politics, but added that she believes it has been worth the cost.

Home Address
101 Blossom
Lake Jackson, Texas 77566
(409) 297-3102

Representative Don Pease (D., Ohio)

Pease, who was elected to the House in 1976, retired in 1992. He now is the distinguished visiting professor at Oberlin College in Ohio.

Pease refunded $40,129 in leftover campaign funds and gave $37,980 to political organizations. He also donated $25,000 to Oberlin College and $130,355 to the Lorain (Ohio) Community Foundation.

Business Address
Oberlin College
Politics Department
Rice Hall #234
Oberlin, Ohio 44074
(216) 775-8487

Representative Claude Pepper (D., Florida)

Pepper was elected to the Senate in 1936 and served until he was defeated in the 1950 Democratic primary by George Smathers. Pepper was elected to the House in 1962. Although Pepper served in the House longer than he had in the Senate, he was always referred to as "Senator Pepper." He died while in office in May 1989.

After his death, $37,353 in leftover campaign funds was transferred to his estate and subsequently distributed to a member of his staff.

Representative Charles Percy (R., Illinois)

Percy, who was elected to the Senate in 1966, was unseated in 1984 by Democrat Paul Simon. Today, Percy lives and works in Washington as the president of Charles Percy & Associates, an international relations and trade consulting firm, and as the chairman and president of the Hariri Foundation. Founded by Lebanon Prime Minister Rafiq Hariri, the foundation brings Lebanese students to the United States and Canada and pays for their educations at colleges and universities in exchange for their agreement to return to Lebanon to devote themselves to rebuilding the country.

As the father-in-law of Senator John D. (Jay) Rockefeller IV (D., West Virginia), Percy told the *Chicago Tribune* that he decided against becoming a lobbyist because "I didn't want to lobby him." He also said that becoming a foreign agent did not appeal to him because "I didn't feel comfortable doing that with all those CIA briefings every morning for 18 years."

Percy says that his consulting company "helps U.S. companies with their trade problems abroad."

Business Address
Charles Percy & Associates
900 19th Street, N.W.
Suite 900
Washington, D.C. 20006
(202) 872-1164
and
Hariri Foundation
1020 19th Street, N.W.
Suite 320
Washington, D.C. 20006
(202) 659-9200

Home Address
1691 34th Street, N.W.
Washington, D.C. 20036
(202) 337-1691

Representative Carl Perkins (D., Kentucky)

Perkins, elected to the House in 1948, died in office on August 3, 1984.

Representative Carl Perkins, Jr. (D., Kentucky)

Perkins was elected to the House in 1984 to fill the vacancy created by the death of his father, Carl Perkins, Sr. He retired in 1992 after it was disclosed that he had 514 overdrafts at the House bank.
Carl Perkins, Jr. could not be located.

Representative Joel Pritchard (R., Washington)

Elected to the House in 1972, Pritchard pledged to serve no more than 12 years and retired in 1984. He is currently the lieutenant governor of Washington.

Business Address
Lieutenant Governor's Office
Legislative Building
Olympia, Washington 98504
(206) 786-7700

Senator William Proxmire (D., Wisconsin)

Proxmire was elected to the Senate in 1957 to fill the vacancy created by the death of Republican Joseph McCarthy. He retired in 1988 and has remained in Washington.
"I'm married to a wonderful woman who was born in Washington," Proxmire said. "She established a business in Washington called Washington Inc., and I'm very proud of her. I really owe her a lot. She did a beautiful job of raising the children."
Today at age 79, Proxmire works out of a small carrel provided to him by the Library of Congress. "I walk to work; it's about six miles," he said. "Before that I do calisthenics for about 45 minutes. Then I'm very careful about my diet." In 1994, he wrote a book, *Your Joy Ride to Health* which he has used to promote his views on health and nutrition.
Proxmire has always had a different view of politics. "Unlike most elected officials, I was anything but a natural people's choice," he wrote in his 1972 book *Uncle Sam: Last of the Big Time Spenders*. "From the beginning I was an outsider, an interloper. I carpetbagged into Wisconsin with about every political liability in the book. I had no degree from the University of Wisconsin. I had one from Yale and two from Harvard, all of which were political liabilities. My last

employment had been not just on Wall Street, but with J.P. Morgan and Company. How do you like that for a 'liberal Democrat?'"

As a prominent critic of money in politics, Proxmire practiced what he preached: he spent just $145 in his last campaign in 1982. He is also prone to attack the institution of Congress.

"After my 31 years as a United States Senator, I believe it's the best job in the world," he recently wrote to the Center. "Yes, it's better than being President or Chief Justice of the Supreme Court, or chairman of the board of any of the country's biggest corporations, a movie star, the commissioner of big league baseball or football or king of the talk show hosts or the presiding officer of Yale or Harvard University of the editor-in-chief of *The New York Times*.

"Here's why: unlike other top executives you can focus on exactly the issues that concern you the most.

"The trouble with the Senate today is that almost every senator believes that the cost of remaining in this marvelous job requires spending a great deal of your time raising money. Even if the money comes in easily through professional fundraisers, just the process of accepting contributions forces you consciously or unconsciously to modify your convictions and vote the way your big contributors want you to vote."

In an interview, Proxmire continued his campaign against big-money politics. He has no sympathy for the lawmakers who complain of burn-out. "They may not tell you this, but they are spending all their time on the goddamn phone raising money," he said. "I like it more since I left, but I've got a new attitude toward life. Your happiness is entirely up to yourself. You can always overcome all of that by simply smiling."

Business Address
Library of Congress
Madison Building
1st and Independence Avenue, S.E.
Washington, D.C. 20540
(202) 479-4065

Home Address
3097 Ordway Street, N.W.
Washington, D.C. 20008

Representative Carl Pursell (R., Michigan)

Elected to the House in 1976, Pursell retired in 1992. Today, he serves on the board of regents of Eastern Michigan University.

Pursell converted $129,000 in leftover campaign funds to personal use.

Business Address
Eastern Michigan University
46200 North Territorial Road
Plymouth, Michigan 48170
(313) 459-3636

Senator Dan Quayle (R., Indiana)

Elected to the House in 1976, Quayle ran for the Senate in 1980 and defeated Birch Bayh, the Democratic incumbent. In 1988 President Bush selected Quayle as his vice presidential running mate. Today, Quayle and his family have returned to Indianapolis, where he is a principal with Circle Investors and is contemplating a Presidential bid in 1996. He authored the 1994 best-selling book, *Standing Firm*. Quayle is chairman of the Hudson Institute's Competitiveness Center.

Business Address
Circle Investors
Capitol Center, South Tower, Suite 350
201 North Illinois Street
Indianapolis, Indiana 46204
(317) 237-3377

Senator Jennings Randolph (D., West Virginia)

Elected to the House in 1932, Randolph served until 1946, when he lost his reelection bid. From 1947 to 1958, Randolph worked as a Washington lobbyist and was elected to the Senate in 1958. He retired in 1984.

Randolph, 92, lives in a nursing care facility in St. Louis to be close to his family.

Representative William Ratchford (D, Connecticut);

Ratchford, who was elected to the House in 1978, was unseated in 1984. He then joined the Washington lobbying firm of Gold & Liebengood, Inc. President Clinton named Ratchford Associate Administrator of Congressional and Government Affairs with the General Services Administration.

Business Address	*Home Address*
General Services Administration	2816 North Jefferson Street
18th and F Street, N.W.	Arlington, Virginia 22207
Washington, D.C. 20405	(703) 241-4989
(202) 501-0563	

Representative Richard Ray (D., Georgia)

Elected to the House in 1982, Ray lost the 1992 election to Republican Mac Collins. Before his election to the House, Ray had served as Senator Sam Nunn's chief of staff from 1972 to 1982.

Ray began his own lobbying and consulting firm in January 1993. According to a brochure, "Richard Ray, Inc. began its first month in business with two of the nation's top 50 firms, Lockheed Inc. and Hughes Aircraft, and has added several quality accounts during its first year of business, including Martin Marietta Corporation, and Gulfstream Aerospace of Savannah, Georgia. . . . Richard Ray is dedicated to providing prompt support and advice on legislative and governmental matters, specializing in defense and environmental policy analysis and federal agencies. Mr. Ray, for 20 years, has been actively involved in and understands the legislative process." He can offer "an established rapport with members and staff of the congressional authorization and appropriation committees as well as the federal agencies."

Ray's stationery and business cards feature a Capitol dome and the words "Richard Ray, Former Member of Congress."

Business Address
Richard Ray, Inc.
P.O. Box 15099
Alexandria, Virginia 22309
(703) 780-0309
and
Richard Ray, Inc.
P.O. Box 1649
Byron, Georgia 31008
(912) 956-4010

Home Address
441 Southwood Drive
Alexandria, Virginia 22309

Representative John Rhodes III (R., Arizona)

Elected to the House in 1986, Rhodes lost the 1992 election to Democrat Sam Coppersmith. He has remained in Washington and is special counsel to the Washington law firm of Hunton & Williams. Rhodes's father, John Rhodes, was the House Republican Leader from 1974 until his retirement in 1982; he also works at Hunton & Williams as counsel.

Rhodes also lobbies for the Central Arizona Project, which every year asks Congress for money for such projects as enlarging the Theodore Roosevelt Dam, completing the Tucson Aqueduct, and replacing rusted water siphons in Tucson.

Business Address
Hunton & Williams
2000 Pennsylvania Avenue, NW, Suite 9000
Washington, D.C. 20006
(202) 955-1500

Home Address
3129 Worthington Street
Washington, D.C. 20015
(202) 362-6461

Representative Frank Riggs (R., California)

Riggs was elected to the House in 1990, defeating Democrat Doug Bosco. He then was defeated by Democrat Dan Hamburg in the 1992 election.

In 1994, Riggs took back the seat from Hamburg. Riggs had operated Duncan Enterprises, a property development and home building company. He also worked for a software company, Learning Tools, until he resigned to run for Congress in 1994.

His 1994 campaign stationary featured an official looking Capitol dome with "Frank Riggs, Member of Congress From 1991-1993, California 1st District."

Business Address   *Home Address*
Duncan Enterprises   155 Merner Drive
155 Merner Drive   Windsor, California 95492
Windsor, California 95492   (707) 838-9128
(707) 838-9095

Representative Matthew Rinaldo (R., New Jersey)

Rinaldo was elected to the House in 1972 and retired in 1992. He served on the House Energy and Commerce Committee and was the ranking Republican on its Telecommunications and Finance Subcommittee.

He is now the president of the International CellularVision Association and the chairman of the Advanced Telecommunications Institute. In March 1994, Rinaldo registered to lobby Congress on telecommunications issues for the International CellularVision Association.

Business Address   *Home Address*
International CellularVision Association   700 New Hampshire Avenue, N.W.
2600 Virginia Avenue, N.W.   Washington, D.C. 20037
Washington, D.C. 20037
(202) 965-4265
and Advanced Telecommunications Institute
Stevens Institute of Technology
Hoboken, New Jersey 07030

Representative Don Ritter (R, Pennsylvania)

Elected to the House in 1978, Ritter lost the 1992 election to Democrat Paul McHale. He has joined Dennis Hertel, another former member of the House, as the co-chairman of the National Environmental Policy Institute. The organization, which is financed by corporate interests, promotes environmental ideas "based on good science, rational risk assessment, and sound economics," according to their brochure.

Home Address
2746 Forest Drive
Coopersburg, Pennsylvania 18036
(215) 282-4947

Representative J. Kenneth Robinson (R., Virginia)

Elected to the House in 1970, Robinson retired in 1984 and returned to his hometown of Winchester, Virginia. He died in 1991.

Representative Tommy Robinson (D., Arkansas)

Robinson was elected to the House as a Democrat in 1984. He switched parties and left the House in 1990 to run for governor of Arkansas but lost the Republican primary to Sheffield Nelson. Today, Robinson is again a Democrat and is living and working on his 7,000-acre farm in Marianna, Arkansas.

Robinson had more in overdrafts at the House bank -- 996 -- than any other lawmaker. His political career seems to be on hold, and his farm is prospering.

"We're having the best financial years in our lives, but we're all working hard," he told the *Memphis Commercial Appeal*. "It's nice to live out in the country, and I had nothing to do with Whitewater. At this moment in time, I'm content, and the Lord has not called me. If I get the call, maybe the spirit will move me."

Home Address
162 Pearl Road
Marianna, Arkansas 72360
(501) 295-6414

Representative Peter Rodino (D., New Jersey)

Elected to the House in 1948, Rodino retired in 1988, after guiding the House Judiciary Committee through the turbulent Watergate years. Rodino, now 85-years-old, is a professor at Seton Hall University and works at the law offices of Rodino & Rodino in East Hanover, New Jersey.

Business Address
Seton Hall University
One Newark Center
Newark, New Jersey 07102

and Rodino & Rodino
11 Eagle Rock Avenue
East Hanover, New Jersey 07936
(201) 887-8882

Representative Buddy Roemer (R., Louisiana)

Elected to the House as a Democrat in 1980, Roemer switched parties, was elected governor of Louisiana and resigned from the House on March 14, 1988. He lost his 1992 reelection bid, however, and now runs the Sterling Group, an international trading company in Baton Rouge, Louisiana.

"You have to plant before you harvest, and that's particularly true in politics -- so get people involved early," Roemer told the National Association of Insurance Women in July 1994. "It isn't esoteric, or amateurish, or a footnote in history for people to get involved in government. I don't know how government will work any other way."

Business Address
The Sterling Group
339 Florida Boulevard
Baton Rouge, Louisiana 70801
(504) 387-9289

Representative Robert Roe (D., New Jersey)

Roe was elected to the House in 1968 and retired in 1992. A former chairman of the Public Works and Transportation Committee, Roe is now a transportation consultant and lobbyist who works for the very public and private interests that benefit from legislation he wrote.

Roe's clients have included Bergen County, New Jersey; the city of Newark; the engineering firm of Edwards and Lecey, Inc.; and Allied Junction Corporation. According to published reports, Bergen County has agreed to pay Roe $75,000 to help it secure federal funds for transportation projects, and Newark is paying him $120,000 for guidance on financing a rail link between Newark International Airport and Elizabeth, New Jersey, and various road projects.

"Say what you want, but he's the man with the juice," Alvin Zak, Newark's chief engineer told the *Bergen County Record*. William "Pat" Schuber, the Bergen County Executive, said that he was "mesmerized" by Roe's knowledge of transportation. "Here is a man with such talent and knowledge that it shouldn't go to waste," Schuber said.

Business Address
Robert Roe Associates
P.O. Box 407
Wayne, New Jersey 07474
(201) 696-2077

Representative John Rowland (R., Connecticut)

Rowland was elected to the House in 1984 and served until 1990, when he left to make an unsuccessful bid for governor of Connecticut. In 1994, he was elected governor.

After Rowland left Congress, he established Rowland Associates, a lobbying firm with offices in Washington and Connecticut that represented United Technologies Corporation (Connecticut's biggest private employer), Textron Lycoming, Inc., and Electric Boat, among others. "We brought John Rowland in because of his relationships in Washington and his knowledge of the process," William McDaniel, a spokesman for Textron Lycoming, told the *Hartford Courant*.

Nynex Corporation, the telecommunications company, also employed Rowland as a lobbyist. Thomas Tauke, another former member of the House, who's now NYNEX's executive vice president, told the Hartford Courant that Rowand was the company's "sounding board on what's going on in Connecticut."

Home Address
925 Oronoke Road
Waterbury, Connecticut 06708
(203) 759-0344

Representative Edward Roybal (D., California)

Roybal was elected to the House in 1962 and retired in 1992. He was replaced in the House by his daughter, Louise Roybal-Allard. Today, he works as a volunteer for the Edward R. Roybal Institute for Applied Gerontology at California State University in Los Angeles.

Business Address
Edward R. Roybal Institute
for Applied Gerontology
5151 State University Drive
Los Angeles, California 90032
(213) 343-4724

Senator Warren Rudman (R., New Hampshire)

Rudman was elected to the Senate in 1980. He retired in 1992 and joined the Washington office of Paul, Weiss, Rifkind, Wharton and Garrison, a New York City-based law firm. Along with former Democratic Senator Paul Tsongas of Massachusetts, Rudman founded the Concord Coalition, which focuses on issues relating to the federal budget deficit. In 1994, President Clinton named Rudman to the President's Foreign Intelligence Advisory Board. He also serves on the board of directors (along with Tsongas) of the Committee for a Responsible Federal Budget.

Business Address
Paul, Weiss, Rifkind, Wharton and Garrison
1615 L Street, N.W. Suite 1300
Washington, D.C. 20036
(202) 223-7300

Representative Eldon Rudd (R., Arizona)

Rudd was elected to the House in 1976 and retired in 1986. When he left the House, he joined the Arizona law firm of Shimmel, Hill, Bishop and Gruender. He retired from the firm in 1994 and now works as a consultant.

Rudd transferred $53,835 in leftover campaign funds to the Eldon Rudd Fund, made $18,078 in payments to his Office of Personnel Management account, and spent approximately $8,700 on other expenses. "Winding it [the committee] all down is a real pain in the neck," he told *Congressional Quarterly*.

Business Address	*Home Address*
Eldon Rudd Consultancy, Inc.	6909 East Main Street
P.O. Box 873	Scottsdale, Arizona 85251
Scottsdale, Arizona 85252	
(602) 947-7203	

Representative Marty Russo (D., Illinois)

Russo was elected to the House in 1974 and served until he lost the 1992 Democratic primary. After he left Congress, Russo joined the lobbying firm of Cassidy and Associates as its director vice chairman. Cassidy and Associates represents AT&T, as well as the Chicago Board of Trade, General Dynamics Corp., Jones Intercable, Inc., Kraft, Inc., the National Cable Television Association, Ocean Spray Cranberries, Inc., and Polaroid Corporation.

Russo was a member of the House Ways and Means Committee. Russo, a close friend of former chairman Dan Rostenkowski, now lobbies his former colleagues on the committee.

Business Address
Cassidy & Associates
700 13th Street, N.W., Fourth Floor
Washington, D.C. 20005
(202) 347-0773

Representative Patricia Saiki (R., Hawaii)

Saiki was elected to the House in 1986. She gave up her seat in 1990 to make an unsuccessful bid for the Senate. In 1991, President Bush named Saiki to head the Small Business Administration. With the end of the Bush Administration, Saiki spent a semester as a teaching fellow at Harvard University's John F. Kennedy School of Government.

She returned to Hawaii in 1993 and announced her candidacy for governor in 1994. "It's an uphill fight and will be an exciting race," Saiki said. "I wouldn't be in it if I didn't think I could win it." Saiki lost the three-way race for governor.

Business Address
1551 Kapiolani Boulevard
Honolulu, Hawaii 96814
(808) 951-5557

Senator Terry Sanford (D., North Carolina)

Sanford was elected to the Senate in 1986. He was defeated in 1992 by Republican Lauch Faircloth. Today, he practices law in North Carolina and is a professor of public policy at Duke University.

Business Address
McNair & Sanford
P.O. Box 2447
Raleigh, North Carolina 27602
(919) 890-4190

Representative Gus Savage (D., Illinois)

Savage was elected to the House in 1980 and served until he was defeated in the 1992 Democratic primary by Mel Reynolds. He now lives in Chicago.

Savage, who was known in the House for his sharp tongue, was also accused of sexually harassing a Peace Corps volunteer while on an official trip to Africa.

Representative Harold Sawyer (R., Michigan)

Sawyer was elected to the House in 1976 to fill his friend Gerald Ford's seat. He served until 1984. Sawyer said that he left his successful law practice to run for the House because he thought that it would be fun serving while his old buddy Ford was president. "I couldn't believe that Ford would lose," Sawyer said.

After eight years in office, Sawyer retired from public life. "I couldn't afford to stay any longer," he said. "I was making almost $300,000 a year and went down [when elected] to $44,000. I was gradually going broke keeping up four cars and two houses."

"It's an awfully frustrating job. You get so much information but you can't do a damn thing. I could do more, change more laws, practicing law. If you are used to calling the shots, which I was, in Congress you can't. It's a whole frustrating picture. I enjoyed it and wouldn't have missed it, but you would have had to pay me to stay another year."

Sawyer said that he was surprised when he went to Washington. "I expected to meet a bunch of political hacks," he said. "But I met a bunch of dedicated, hardworking and intelligent people."

Today, Sawyer and his wife live in a small house on 60 acres, complete with a fishing pond and deer, near Grand Rapids. He practices law with the Grand Rapids firm of Sawyer and Sawyer and travels with his wife.

Business Address
Sawyer and Sawyer
510 Grand Plaza Place
220 Lyon Street, N.W.
Grand Rapids, Michigan 49503
(616) 451-8478

Home Address
4100 14 Mile Road
Rockford, Michigan 49341
(606) 866-1944

Representative Bill Schuette (R., Michigan)

Elected to the House in 1984, Schuette gave up his seat in 1990 to make an unsuccessful bid for the Senate. After the 1990 general election, Schuette was appointed to be the director of the Michigan Department of Agriculture by Governor John Engler. He resigned that position in February 1994 to return to his former law firm of Currie and Kendall in Midland, Michigan.

Business Address
Currie and Kendall
6024 Eastman Avenue
Midland, Michigan 48640
(517) 839-0300

Representative Richard Schulze (R., Pennsylvania)

Schulze, who was elected to the House in 1974, retired in 1992. After leaving the House, Schulze joined Valis Associates, a Washington-based lobbying firm as a senior legislative adviser.

Business Address
Valis Associates
1747 Pennsylvania Ave., N.W.
Suite 850
Washington, D.C. 20006
(202) 833-5055

Home Address
1600 North Oak Street, #1220
Arlington, Virginia 22209
(703) 524-2424

Representative Claudine Schneider (R., Rhode Island)

Schneider was elected to the House in 1980, where she served until she made an unsuccessful bid to unseat Democratic Senator Claiborne Pell in 1990.

Today, Schneider lives in Washington, where she works for Renew America, an environmental group. In 1994, President Clinton appointed Schneider to the Competitiveness Policy Council. She has also founded the Artemis Foundation, an organization that promotes the conservation of biodiversity.

Business Address
Renew America
1400 16th Street, N.W.
Washington, D.C. 20036
(202) 232-6026

Home Address
641 Acker Place, N.E.
Washington, D.C. 20002
(202) 546-7780

Representative James Scheuer (D., New York)

Scheuer served in the House from 1964 until 1972, when he was defeated. He was reelected in 1974 and served until he retired in 1992. In 1994, President Clinton appointed Scheuer to be the U.S. director of the European Bank for Reconstruction and Development.

Home Address
2435 Tracy Place
Washington, D.C. 20008
(202) 232-5776

Representative John Seiberling (D., Ohio)

Seiberling was elected to the House in 1970 and served until his retirement in 1986. Today, he practices law in Akron, Ohio.

Home Address
2370 Martin Road
Akron, Ohio 44333

Senator John Seymour (R., California)

Seymour was appointed to the Senate in 1991 to fill out the term of Republican Pete Wilson who'd become Governor of California. In 1992, he was defeated in the general election by Democrat Dianne Feinstein. Wilson then appointed Seymour to head the California Housing Finance Authority.

Business Address
California Housing Finance Agency
1121 L Street
Sacramento, California 95814
(916) 324-4638

Representative James Shannon (D., Massachusetts)

Elected to the House in 1978, Shannon gave up his seat in 1984 to run for the Senate, but lost the Democratic primary to John Kerry. Today, he works as the vice president and general counsel of the National Fire Protection Association.

Business Address
National Fire Protection Association
One Batterymarch Park
Quincy, Massachusetts 02269
(617) 984-7235

Representative Norman Shumway (R., California)

Shumway was elected to the House in 1978. He pledged to serve no more than six terms and retired from Congress in 1990. After he returned to California, Shumway became a member of the California Public Utilities Commission.

Business Address
Public Utilities Commission
505 Van Ness Avenue, Rm. 5213
San Francisco, California 94102
(415) 703-1407

Representative Gerry Sikorski (D., Minnesota)

Elected to the House in 1982, Sikorski lost the 1992 general election after it was disclosed that he'd had 697 overdrafts at the House Bank. Today, Sikorski is the director of public affairs for Schatz, Paquin, Lockridge, Grindal and Holstein, a Washington law and lobbying firm.

Business Address
Schatz, Paquin, Lockridge, Grindal and Holstein
1301 K Street, N.W. #650
Washington, D.C. 20005
(202) 789-3970

Representative Mark Siljander (R., Michigan)

Just 28 years old when he was elected to the House in a 1981 special election to succeed David Stockman, who gave up the seat to become the director of the Office of Management and Budget in the Reagan Administration, Siljander served until he lost the 1986 Republican primary to Fred Upton.

In an unusual twist, Siljander ran for the House again in 1992. However, this time he ran for a Virginia seat and lost in the primary.

Siljander said that he's lived in Virginia since his election to the House and that three of his four children were born in the state. Today, he doubts that he will run again for Congress. "It's not something that I need to do for my resume," he said.

Following his first loss in 1986, Siljander worked as the Deputy U.S. Representative to the United Nations for one year. He now runs Global Strategies, an international trade consulting group in Great Falls, Virginia.

Home Address
650 Keithly Road
Great Falls, Virginia 22066
(703) 450-2900

Representative Paul Simon (D., Illinois)

Simon was elected to the House in 1974. He unseated Republican Senator Charles Percy in 1984 and currently is in his second term in the Senate. On November 15, 1994, he announced that he will retire at the end of his current term.

Business Address
426 Dirksen Senate Office Building
Washington, D.C. 20510
(202) 224-2152

Representative D. French Slaughter (R., Virginia)

Slaughter was elected to the House in 1984 and served until he resigned for health reasons in 1991. He lives in Culpepper, Virginia.

Representative Lawrence Smith (D., Florida)

Smith who was elected to the House in 1982 retired in 1992 after it was disclosed that he'd had 161 overdrafts at the House bank. Smith was also accused of using campaign funds to pay gambling debts and pleaded guilty to income tax evasion in May 1993. He served a three-month sentence in the Dade County Metropolitan Correctional Center a minimum security facility, in late 1993.

Today, Smith works as a lobbyist with the Cuban American Foundation. In June 1994, he was accused of abusing his Democratic cloakroom privileges for lobbying. Such privileges are provided to all former members. Speaker Thomas Foley took the unusual step of announcing from the rostrum that former members may not use their privileges if they engage in lobbying on the floor or in the cloakrooms.

"If I did anything wrong, it was inadvertent," Smith told the Associated Press. "I don't think it can be me that's the big offender. What I have to say can be said anywhere."

After Smith left the House, he landed a three-month, $18,624 consulting contract with the House Administration Committee for conducting a survey and review of the House restaurant.

Smith spent $76,565 in leftover campaign funds on legal fees resulting from his conviction.

Business Address
Government Relations
3111 Sterling Road
Ft. Lauderdale, Florida 33312

Home Address
3511 North 52nd Avenue
Hollywood, Florida 33021

Representative Virginia Smith (R., Nebraska)

Elected to the House in 1974, Smith retired in 1990. Today, she spends her winters in Sun City West, Arizona, and summers in Nebraska. Still active in public affairs, Smith made news during the summer of 1994 when she successfully lobbied for a new U.S. Post Office to be built in Sun City West. Senator Dennis DeConcini of Arizona told the *Arizona Republic*, "When a Congressman questioned why should he approve this, I said, 'Virginia Smith.'"

Home Address
P. O. Box 643
Chappell, Nebraska 69139
(308) 874-3292

Representative Peter Smith (R., Vermont)

Smith, who was elected to the House in 1988, lost the 1990 election to Bernard Sanders. He remained in Washington as dean of education and human development at the George Washington University, and in January 1995, became founding president of California State University at Monterey Bay.
See chapter "Starting Over: Peter Smith."

Business Address
California State University
  at Monterey Bay
(408) 393-3330

Home Address
3607 North Piedmont Street
Arlington, Virginia 22207
(703) 522-6322

Representative Denny Smith (R., Oregon)

Elected to the House in 1980 when he upset Representative Al Ullman, chairman of the House Ways and Means Committee, Smith served until he lost the 1990 election.

Smith returned to Oregon and worked as the chairman of Eagle Newspapers, Inc., which owns 20 newspapers and printing plants in three states. In 1994, he lost a bid to become the governor of Oregon. He is the son of former Oregon Governor Elmo Smith.

Business Address
Eagle Newspapers, Inc.
P. O. Box 12008
Salem, Oregon 97302
(503) 393-1774

Home Address
3541 El Dorado Loop South
Salem, Oregon 97302
(503) 362-2337

Representative Robert Smith (R., New Hampshire)

Smith was elected to the House in 1984 and to the Senate in 1990. He currently serves in the Senate.

Business Address
332 Dirksen Senate Office Building
Washington, D.C. 20510
(202) 224-2841

Representative Gene Snyder (R., Kentucky)

After serving one term in the House (from 1963 to 1965). Snyder was elected again in 1966 and he served until he retired in 1986 and returned to Kentucky.

"Franklin Roosevelt gave us the New Deal; Harry Truman gave us the Square Deal; now Clinton's giving us the Raw Deal," Snyder said on his answering machine recording. "So we're out picking up aluminum cans, trying to get enough money to pay our taxes, so please leave a message and I'll get back to you."

Snyder, who converted $173,202 in leftover campaign funds to personal use, told the *Louisville Courier-Journal*, "I don't think it's any of your business what I am going to do with it. I'm not a public figure."

Home Address
110 Maple Avenue
Pewee Valley, Kentucky 40056
(502) 241-0455

Representative Stephen Solarz (D., New York)

Solarz, who was elected to the House in 1974 was defeated in the 1992 Democratic primary by Nydia Velazquez after it was disclosed that he'd had 743 overdrafts at the House bank.

In 1993, President Clinton appointed Solarz to be the Ambassador to India. When Solarz' FBI clearance was held up for months, however, he withdrew his nomination. Clinton subsequently named Solarz to be the chairman of the new Central Asian American Enterprise Fund, which is designed to encourage investments in Kazakhstan, Kyrgyzstan, Uzbekistan, Tajikistan, and Turkmenistan.

Solarz used $197,376 in leftover campaign funds to pay for legal fees.

Home Address
1120 Bellview Road
McLean, Virginia 22102
(703) 759-3326

Representative Arlen Stangeland (R., Minnesota)

Stangeland was elected to the House in 1977 in a special election. He lost the 1990 general election to Colin Peterson after the *St. Cloud (Minn.) Times* reported that Stangeland had made 341 telephone calls -- charged to his office credit card -- to a woman named Eva Jarvis. Stangeland, a married father of seven, denied a romance.

Stangeland now lives in Pelican Rapids, Minnesota, and says that he works as a consultant and lobbyist about four days a month. "Retirement is really great," he said. "Wouldn't trade it for anything. I enjoyed my term, but I wouldn't go back to it."

Home Address
Route #3, Box 235
Pelican Rapids, Minnesota 56572
(218) 863-6434

Representative Harley Staggers (D., West Virginia)

Staggers was elected to the House in 1984 and served until 1992, when he lost the Democratic primary to Alan Mollohan. He has returned to his law practice in Keyser, West Virginia.

Business Address
Staggers, Staggers & Webb
P.O. Box 876
Keyser, West Virginia 26726
(304) 788-5749

Representative Richard Stallings (D., Illinois)

Stallings who was elected to the House in 1984 gave up his seat in 1992 to make an unsuccessful bid for the Senate. In November 1993, he was sworn in as an U.S. Nuclear Waste Negotiator, an independent federal agency that works to find states or Indian reservations as hosts for facilities to house spent nuclear fuel.

Business Address
Nuclear Waste Negotiator
1823 Jefferson Place, N.W.
Washington, D.C. 20036
(202) 634-6244

Senator Robert Stafford (R., Vermont)

Stafford was elected to the House in 1960 and to the Senate in 1970. He retired from the Senate in 1988 and returned to Vermont.

He now is an honorary professor of public affairs at Castleton College in Vermont and remains active in the efforts to control the use of the filibuster in the Senate.

Home Address
Sugarwood Hill Road
R.R. 1, Box 3954
Rutland, Vermont 05702
(802) 773-1620

Senator John Stennis (D., Mississippi)

Stennis served in the Senate from 1947 until his retirement in 1988. He now lives in a retirement home in Mississippi.

Home Address
Siena Center
St. Catherine's Village
Madison, Mississippi 39110

Representative Fernand St Germain (D., Rhode Island)

St Germain was elected to the House in 1960. He lost the 1988 election just weeks after the Justice Department found what it called "substantial evidence of serious and sustained misconduct" in St Germain's role as the chairman of the House Banking, Finance, and Urban Affairs Committee.

He now lives in Florida and refused an interview request. "I live a private life and I'd like to keep it like that," he said.

St Germain converted $249,924 in leftover campaign funds to personal use, including $92,500 to pay legal bills related to the Ethics Committee and Justice Department investigations.

Business Address
TransWorld
1200 Eton Court, N.W.
Washington, D.C. 20007
(202) 625-6100

Home Address
1 Beach Drive
St. Petersburg, Florida 33701

Representative Samuel Stratton (D., New York)

Stratton who was elected to the House in 1958, retired for health reasons in 1988 and died on September 3, 1990. Before his death, Stratton converted $198,795 in leftover campaign funds to personal use.

Representative Mike Strang (R., Colorado)

Strang was elected to the House in from 1984 and was unseated in 1986 by Democrat Ben Nighthorse Campbell. He returned to Colorado and is a rancher and consultant on natural resources.

Home Address
Mill Iron Lazy M Ranch
0393 County Road 102
Carbondale, Colorado 81623
(303) 963-2319

Representative Fofo Sunia (D., American Samoa)

Elected to the House in 1980, Sunia resigned in September 1988 after he pleaded guilty in a federal payroll fraud case involving his congressional office. His administrative assistant went to jail. Today, Sunia lives in American Samoa.

Business Address
American Samoa Government
Pongo Pongo
American Samoa 96799

Representative Mac Sweeney (R., Texas)

Sweeney who was elected to the House in 1984 lost the 1988 reelection bid in 1988. Just 29 years old when he went to the House, Sweeney was investigated during his first term for abusing his congressional franking privilege and allegedly ordering staff members to work on his reelection campaign. He was cited for "deficiencies in office management" by the House Standards of Official Conduct Committee.

After the left the House, Sweeney returned to Texas, moved his wife and two small children into his in-law's home, and finished law school. He could not be located.

Representative Pat Swindall (R., Georgia)

Swindall was elected to the House in 1984. Swindall lost the 1988 election to Democrat Ben Jones. After he was indicted for his role in a money laundering operation, he was convicted in 1989 of perjury for lying to a federal grand jury investigating the money scheme and was fined $30,000 and sentenced to one year in prison. Three counts of the conviction were later overturned, but the Supreme Court refused in January 1994, to overturn the remaining six counts.

On February 11, 1994, Swindell drove himself to an Atlanta prison to begin his sentence. "I told my children last night that Joseph went to prison for 13 years because he refused to obey Potiphar's wife," Swindall told *The Atlanta Constitution*. "I wouldn't do what the government wanted me to do." He also joked that his imprisonment was a conspiracy between Planned Parenthood and the government to prevent he and his wife, Kim, from having more children. "This is the only way my wife and I have got to stop having kids," he said. The Swindalls have seven children, ages three to nine.

A lawyer before entering Congress, Swindall was forced to surrender his law license and worked in real estate and flea market management after his conviction.

Home Address
543 Mont Eagle Trace
Stone Mountain, Georgia 30087
(404) 469-3850

Senator Steve Symms (R., Idaho)

Symms was elected to the House in 1972 and to the Senate in 1980 when he unseated Democrat Frank Church. He retired from the Senate in 1992.

He told States News Service that he spends about "two-thirds of my time here [in Washington] and one-third in Idaho," adding, "Eventually, I'd like to reverse that." In Washington, Symms runs the lobbying firm Symms and Lehn Associates and works as the president of the Freedom Alliance, Oliver North's former policy group.

In Idaho, Symms works on his family's Sunny Slope Ranch and is a director of the Albertson's supermarket chain.

Business Address	*Home Address*
Symms, Lehn & Associates, Inc.	7510 Crossgate Lane
210 Cameron Street	Alexandria, Virginia 22310
Alexandria, Virginia 22314	(703) 719-9856

Representative Robin Tallon (S., South Carolina)

Tallon was elected to the House in 1982 and retired in 1992. Tallon then joined the Washington-based Tobacco Institute as a senior consultant. The FBI investigated Tallon for possible lobbying violations in 1993, after he visited his successor in the House, James Clyburn. He was not charged.

Lobbying "is something that certainly I'm going to give some thought to," Tallon told *Roll Call*. "But I have to see what I'm comfortable with and what the Tobacco Institute is comfortable with." Now that the one-year ban is over, Tallon says that he is happy. "It's nice not to have that restriction looming over you," he told *Congressional Quarterly*. "My best friends are members of Congress."

Business Address
Tobacco Institute
1875 I Street, N.W.
Suite 800
Washington, D.C. 20006
(202) 457-4800

Representative Thomas Tauke (R., Iowa)

Tauke who was elected to the House in 1978, gave up his seat in 1990 to make an unsuccessful bid for the Senate. Today, he is the executive vice president for government affairs of NYNEX.

Business Address
NYNEX
Government Affairs
1300 I Street, N.W., #400 West
Washington, D.C. 20005
(202) 336-7901

Representative Gene Taylor (R., Missouri)

Taylor was elected to the House in 1972. He retired in 1988 and returned to his hometown of Sarcoxie, Missouri, where he founded the Gene Taylor Library and Museum. The museum features memorabilia from Taylor's political career and local history and artworks.

Taylor donated $52,811 in leftover campaign funds to the museum. He also converted another $345,044 to personal use. "I haven't done anything wrong," he told *The New York Times* in 1989. "I do a lot of things for public service and I'm going to use some of it for that."

According to his wife, Taylor now works on his farm and runs some cattle. "It isn't the pressure he had before," she said.

Business Address
Gene Taylor Library and Museum
Sarcoxie, Missouri 64862
(417) 548-6130

Representative Robert L. Thomas (D., Georgia)

Thomas, who was elected to the House in 1982, retired in 1992 to become senior vice president for external relations of the Atlanta Committee for the 1996 Summer Olympic Games.

Business Address
Atlanta Committee Olympic Games
P.O. Box 1996
Atlanta, Georgia 30301
(404) 224-1996

Home Address
Grace Acres Farm
Screven, Georgia 31560

Senator John Tower (R., Texas)

Tower, who was elected to the Senate in a 1961 special election to fill the vacancy created when Lyndon Johnson became vice president, retired in 1988. President Bush nominated him to be Secretary of Defense in 1989, but his nomination had to be withdrawn because of congressional pressure. Tower was killed in an airplane crash in South Carolina in April 1991.

Representative Bob Traxler (D., Michigan)

Traxler, who was elected to the House in 1974, retired in 1992 after it was disclosed that he'd had 201 overdrafts at the House bank. Known for his ability to direct government programs and spending to his district, Traxler delivered a $20 million environmental research center to Saginaw and a $1 million renovation for an auditorium in Ypsilanti.

Just one week before he announced his retirement from the House, Traxler held a fund-raiser. At the time, he promised not to keep the campaign funds for his personal use and told *Roll Call*, "If you think that was a factor in my decision [to retire], then you're grossly mistaken."

Traxler, however, converted $295,750 in leftover campaign funds to personal use and gave $5,800 to his campaign for a trustee position at Michigan State University.

Business Address	*Home Address*
Michigan State University	4800 Appletree Lane
Administration Building	Bay City, Michigan 48706
East Lansing, Michigan 48824	(517) 684-2381
(517) 353-4647	

Senator Paul Trible (R., Virginia)

Trible was elected to the House in 1976 and to the Senate in 1982. In 1988, he retired from the Senate at age 42, instead of facing popular Democratic Governor Chuck Robb in a tough Senate race.

Today, Trible is the president of the Jefferson Group, a Washington-based lobbying firm. In 1994, the Jefferson Group attempted a merger with another Washington lobbying firm, Linton, Mields, Reisler & Cotton. When the merger talks fell apart, Trible told *Legal Times* that "Not every initiative works out as you hope it might." The Jefferson Group reportedly has around $6 million in annual billings.

Business Address
The Jefferson Group
1341 G. Street, N.W.
Suite 1100
Washington, D.C. 20005
(202) 638-3535

Senator Paul Tsongas (D., Massachusetts)

Tsongas was elected to the House in 1974 and to the Senate in 1978. Tsongas announced his retirement in 1984 after just one term, because of health concerns and his battle with cancer. With his strength regained, Tsongas made an unsuccessful bid for the Democratic presidential nomination in 1992.

Along with former Republican Senator Warren Rudman, Tsongas is active in the Committee for a Responsible Federal Budget. Rudman and Tsongas also cofounded the Concord Coalition in 1993 and serve as co-chairmen of the organization. In 1994, Tsongas was hired by the Health Care Leadership Council, a group of hospital, pharmaceutical, and insurance company officers to promote health care reform.

Tsongas told the *Dallas Morning News* in March 1994 about his own health and insurance. "I'm covered by my law firm," he said. "Part of the reason I joined a big law firm, besides the money, was that I could get covered. So I had access to both life insurance after a waiting period and health insurance. I've been covered. We had switched to an HMO, so I know what it's like to find a new doctor and establish a new relationship."

Business Address
Foley, Hoag & Elliott
1 Post Office Square
17th Floor
Boston, Massachusetts 02109
(617) 482-1392

Representative Morris Udall (D., Arizona)

Elected to the House in 1960, Udall resigned in May 1991 for health reasons. Stricken in 1980 with Parkinson's disease, Udall battled the disease until a fall in January 1991 put him in the hospital and he could not regain his strength.

Slightly more than $56,000 in leftover campaign funds were turned over to a legal guardian for Udall. His former wife, Patricia "Sam" Udall, lost a 1994 case before the Arizona Court of Appeals in which she attempted to receive a portion of Udall's federal retirement benefits.

Home Address
1812 South 24th Street
Arlington, Virigina 22202
(703) 553-8565

Representative Tom Vandergriff (D., Texas)

Vandergriff was elected to the House in 1982 by just 344 votes but lost his bid for reelection in 1984 to Republican Dick Armey.

"Before I went to Congress, I had many business interests and I continued to pursue and maintain them," Vandergriff said. In 1990, Vandergriff switched political parties and was elected County Judge (county administrator) of Tarrant County, Texas. "I was fortunate enough to be elected and have been serving in that capacity since January 1, 1991," he said. "I am unopposed this year [1994] for re-election to a second four-year term."

Business Address
County Administration Bldg.
100 East Weatherford Street
Fort Worth, Texas 76196
(817) 884-1441

Representative Guy Vander Jagt (R., Michigan)

Vander Jagt who was elected to the House in 1966, was defeated in the 1992 Republican primary by Peter Hoekstra. *The Wall Street Journal* reported that Vander Jagt is the "former member who can't go home again because home -- in Mr. Vander Jagt's case, rural Luther, Michigan -- isn't really home at all."

Vander Jagt chaired the National Republican Congressional Committee (NRCC) for 18 years and left the committee in 1992 with a $4.5 million debt. After he left the House, Vander Jagt created his own political action committee, the National Republican Campaign Committee for Change. This angered a number of Republican leaders, including Representative Bill Paxon, Vander Jagt's successor at the NRCC.

"It's an outrageous attempt to take advantage of the good name of the party," Paxon said in 1994. "It's very clear that if people who previously received a solicitation from the NRCC now get one from the NRCCC, signed by the former chairman of the NRCC, it will cause confusion about who is soliciting money for what."

Vander Jagt again became controversial in 1994 when he signed a letter for the National Smokers Alliance and urged voters in California "to preserve your right to smoke." He is of counsel with the Washington law firm of Baker & Hostetler.

Business Address
Baker & Hostetler
1050 Connecticut Avenue, N.W.
Suite 1100
Washington, D.C. 20036
(202) 861-1722

Representative Doug Walgren (D., Pennsylvania)

Walgren was elected to the House in 1976 but lost in 1990 after his opponent, Republican Rick Santorum, ran a campaign ad featuring Walgren's home in McLean, Virginia. Walgren has remained in Washington and serves as a director of the U.S.-China Chamber of Commerce.

Home Address
8312 Hunting Hill Lane
McLean, Virginia 22102
(703) 893-2564

Representative Alton Waldon (D., New York)

Waldon was elected to the House on July 29, 1986, in a special election to fill the vacancy created by the death of Democrat Joseph Addabbo. He lost his reelection bid in November 1986. He is now a state senator in New York.

Home Address
115-103 22nd Street
Cambria Heights, New York 11411
(718) 723-6136

Representative Wes Watkins (D., Oklahoma)

Watkins was elected to the House in 1976 and served until 1990, when he left to make an unsuccessful bid for Governor. A member of the Appropriations Committee, Watkins became a lobbyist in the Washington firm of Fleishman-Hillard, Inc. In 1994, Watkins ran for governor of Oklahoma as an independent, but lost. He called for a "declaration of independence" from "political bickering and scandal" during his campaign.

Watkins told *Time* magazine that a friend once offered an insight into Washington. "There are some that go to the Capitol and grow," he said, "and some that go there and swell."

Home Address
12 Brentwood Drive
Stillwater, Oklahoma 74075
(405) 624-2222

Representative James Weaver (D., Oregon)

Weaver, who was elected to the House in 1974, gave up his seat in 1986 to make an unsuccessful bid for the Senate. Weaver, a writer and ardent environmentalist, lives in Eugene, Oregon.

Home Address
1601 Olive Street, #1110
Eugene, Oregon 97401
(503) 485-3978

Representative Vin Weber (R., Minnesota)

Weber, who was elected to the House in 1980 retired in 1992 after it was disclosed that he'd had 125 overdrafts at the House bank. Today, Weber is the president of the Washington-based conservative group, Empower America. He also runs his own lobbying firm, The Weber Group, and is a regular political commentator on National Public Radio.

Business Address
The Weber Group
1020 16th Street, N.W. #300
Washington, D.C. 20036
(202) 862-6452

Senator Lowell Weicker (R., Connecticut)

Weicker was elected to the House in 1968 and to the Senate in 1970. He lost his 1988 re-election bid to Joseph Lieberman. However, in 1990, Weicker was elected Governor of Connecticut as an Independent candidate. He retired in 1994 and became the Chief Executive Officer of the Bethesda, Maryland-based health care consulting group of Dresing, Lierman and Weicker. The firm also runs a direct mail pharmacy and direct mail marketing business. Weicker also teaches a course in political science at George Washington University in Washington.

Business Address
Dresing, Lierman and Weicker
6931 Arlington Road, Suite 501
Bethesda, Maryland 20814
(301) 215-7301

Representative Ted Weiss (D., New York)

Weiss was elected to the House in 1976. He died in office in 1992.

Representative Charles Whitley (D., North Carolina)

Elected to the House in 1976, Whitley retired in 1986. He is now a consultant and lobbyist to the Tobacco Institute in Washington. In 1994, Whitley lobbied the Hill on legislation concerning smoking and tobacco regulations.

Business Address
Tobacco Institute
1875 I Street, N.W.
Washington, D.C. 20006
(202) 457-4800

Representative Robert Whittaker (R., Kansas)

Whittaker was elected to the House in 1978. He retired in 1990 and now works as a lobbyist with the Washington firm of Fleishman-Hillard, Inc..

Business Address
Fleishman-Hillard, Inc.
1301 Connecticut Avenue, N.W.
Washington, D.C. 20036
(202) 659-0330

Home Address
2008 Palmer Court
Lawrence, Kansas 66047
(913) 842-4460

Representative G. William Whitehurst (R., Virginia)

Whitehurst was elected to the House in 1968. He retired in 1986. He now works at Old Dominion University where he holds an academic chair and as Kaufman Lecturer in Public Affairs.

"I served in a remarkable transition period in the Congress of the United States," Whitehurst wrote. "When I went to the House of Representatives in 1968, that body was much the same as it had been for the previous 40 years. The seniority system was still in place and one still observed the late Speaker Sam Rayburn's advice of "To get along, go along." That changed with Watergate and the movement for "reform" that ensued in the House. It broke the back of the seniority system and created a legislative body with less cohesion than before.

"The proliferation of political action committees, from some 600 in the early 1970's to over 4,000 by the time my last term ended in 1987, further fractured the House and weakened the discipline that heretofore had generally held. The House, in my judgement, became a less effective legislative body. Friction with the Executive Branch, much of it partisan inspired by both sides of the aisle and the two branches, led to posturing and irresponsibility in managing national affairs, particularly the budget.

"In my last few terms, I found myself wishing that we had a parliamentary system where responsibility for policy and actions are clearly fixed. I did not retire from Congress for these reasons alone. My principal basis for leaving was a life one, a desire to have more personal time with my family. I felt honored to have served for 18 years and to have made a difference for my district and many hundreds of its people individually, but I left with misgivings about our nation's future. The Congress needs to reexamine itself and undertake basic reform measures if it is to recover its ability to deal meaningfully with national problems.

Business Address
Old Dominion University
Norfolk, Virginia 23529
(804) 683-6018

Home Address
401 College Place
Apartment 26
Norfolk, Virginia 23510

Representative Lyle Williams (R., Ohio)

Williams was elected to the House in 1978. He lost the 1984 general election to James Traficant. Williams was named as a co-conspirator in the case of defense contractor Edward Krishack. Williams testified that as Krishack's lobbyist, he never carried money from Krishack to another Ohio Representative Buz Lukens.

"To my knowledge, I never delivered a check to Buz Lukens," Williams testified. "There's no conspiracy here. Buz Lukens had absolutely no ability in my opinion, sir, to help anybody. He couldn't help himself. It's a sad story." Krishack and Williams were subsequently acquitted.

Home Address
2061 Lyntz Towlin Road
Warren, Ohio 44481

Senator Pete Wilson (R., California)

Wilson was elected to the Senate in 1982. He resigned in 1990 after he was elected Governor of California. He was reelected in 1994.

Business Address
Office of the Governor
State Capitol
Sacramento, California 95814

Representative Larry Winn, Jr. (R., Kansas)

Winn was elected to the House in 1966. He retired in 1984 and lives in Shawnee, Kansas.

Home Address
8420 Roe Avenue
Shawnee, Kansas 66207
(913) 642-5449

Senator Timothy Wirth (D., Colorado)

Wirth was elected to the House in 1974. In 1986, he was elected to the Senate where he served for one term. President Clinton named Wirth Undersecretary of State for Global Affairs in 1993.

Home Address
3125 35th Street, N.W.
Washington, D.C. 20016
(202) 244-7179

Representative Howard Wolpe (D., Michigan)

Wolpe was elected to the House in 1978. He retired in 1992 and returned to Michigan where he served as a Distinguished Visiting Professor at Western Michigan University and the Institute of Public Policy at the University of Michigan. Wolpe made an unsuccessful bid for Governor of Michigan in 1994.

Representative George Wortley (R., New York)

Wortley, who was elected to the House in 1980, retired in 1988. He was a lobbyist with the Washington-based firm of Dierman, Wortley & Zola. "I don't do much lobbying on the Hill," Wortley said. "I've been there on business, maybe three or four times in the last four years. Most of my business now involves foreign investment and foreign trade." The firm is a registered foreign agent.

Wortley said that most of his business is focused on China and Taiwan. "Prior to this," he said "I started doing some things in Russia but there were some problems with political currency."

On a personal basis, Wortley said that he is happy to be out of Congress. "I sincerely miss Congress. No place in the world like it. But I'm going to live a lot longer and have a lot better life being out of Congress." Wortley suffered a heart attack in 1989. "I probably would have died, if I had still been in," he said. "In the House, I never had enough time to focus. I didn't control my schedule at all. Everybody wanted a piece of me. Now I'm enjoying a good life."

Business Address   *Home Address*
Dierman, Wortley & Zola   624 Orton Avenue
1350 Eye Street, N.W.   Fort Lauderdale, Florida 33304
Washington, D.C. 20005   (305) 565-0042
(202) 962-9510

Representative Jim Wright (D., Texas)

Wright was elected to the House in 1954 and became Speaker of the House in 1987. He resigned from the House under pressure in June 1989 after the Committee on Standards of Official Conduct found that he had violated House rules by accepting gifts from a business associate and that the royalty plans for his book, *Reflections of a Public Man,* was an attempt to evade the House's limits on outside income.

Wright returned to Fort Worth, Texas, with his wife, Betty. As a former speaker, Wright has a fully staffed government office as part of his retirement privileges. "Briefly put," Wright said, "I have published a book, *Worth it all: My war for Peace*; have written a weekly column for the *Fort Worth Star Telegram*; have been teaching one course at Texas Christian University; and have pursued business interests with American Income Life Insurance Company and Arch Petroleum."

In December 1991, doctors discovered that Wright had a malignant tumor at the base of his tongue. Following surgery, he went through months of radiation and subsequent speech therapy. Wright became one of 400 participants in testing an experimental cancer drug, cisretinoic acid.

Today, Wright lives cancer free. "Betty is convinced I'm going to live longer from having left and come back home," Wright told the *Fort Worth Star Telegram*. "In Washington, it was like I was trying to juggle six balls in the air, and someone throws another one at me. It was just a constant shuffling of priorities. Today, I take it more in stride. I do a lot, but I have time to do it."

Wright converted approximately $388,000 in leftover campaign funds to personal use, including $354,257 in the House Committee on Standards of Official Conduct probe. He used another estimated $34,000 to pay for expenses from June 1989 through June 1992.

Business Address
9A10 Lanham Federal Building
819 Taylor Street
Fort Worth, Texas 76102
(817) 334-3361

Representative Chalmers Wylie (R., Ohio)

Wylie who was elected to the House in 1966, retired in 1992 after it was disclosed that he'd had 515 overdrafts at the House bank. He returned to Ohio, where he works as counsel for the law firm of Emens, Kegler, Brown, Hill and Ritter. He also is an adjunct professor of public policy and management at Ohio State University.

Business Address
Emens, Kegler, Brown, Hill and Ritter
65 East State Street
Columbus, Ohio 43215
(614) 462-5400

Representative Gus Yatron (D., Pennsylvania)

Yatron was elected to the House in 1968. He retired in 1992 and returned to Reading, Pennsylvania.

Home Address
1908 Hessian Road
Reading, Pennsylvania 19602
(215) 376-9123

Representative Robert Young (D., Missouri)

Young was elected to the House in 1976. He was defeated in the 1986 election by Republican Jack Beuchner. A former pipefitter and union activist, Young returned to Missouri after his defeat where, according to his wife, he does "some lobbying on the side."

Young converted approximately $21,500 in leftover campaign money to pay for various expenses, including meals, airfare, moving, and travel.

Home Address
12248 Turkey Creek Court
Maryland Heights, Missouri 63043
(314) 878-8100

Representative Edward Zorinsky (D., Nebraska)

Zorinsky was elected to the Senate in 1976. He died in office on March 6, 1987.

Representative Ed Zschau (R., California)

Zschau, who was elected to the House in 1982, gave up the seat in 1986 to make an unsuccessful bid to unseat Democrat Alan Cranston.

Zschau currently is the vice president and general manager of the storage systems division of the IBM Corporation. He is also involved in a drive to raise funds for the construction of an expansion to the Tech Museum of Innovation in San Jose, California.

Business Address
IBM Corporation
5600 Cottle Road
Building 12
San Jose, California 95193
(408) 256-5690

Epilogue

Members Who Retired

House of Representatives

Douglas Applegate, D-Ohio
Jim Bacchus, D-Fla.
Butler Derrick, D-S.C.
Don Edwards, D-Calif.
Hamilton Fish, R-N.Y.
William D. Ford, D-Mich.
William J. Hughes, D-N.J.
Earl Hutto, D-Fla.
Mike Kopetski, D-Ore.
Tom Lewis, R-Fla.
Marilyn Lloyd, D-Tenn.
Romano Mazzoli, D-Ky.
Alfred A. McCandless, R-Calif.
J. Alex McMillan, R-N.C.
Robert H. Michel, R-Ill.
Austin J. Murphy, D-Pa.
Stephen L. Neal, D-N.C.
Timothy J. Penny, D-Minn.
J.J. Pickle, D-Texas
J. Roy Rowland, D-Ga.
George Sangmeister, D-Ill.
Phillip R. Sharp, D-Ind.
Robert F. Smith, R-Ore.
Al Swift, D-Wash.
Tim Valentine, D-N.C.
Jamie L. Whitten, D-Miss.

Senate

John C. Danforth, R-Mo.
Dennis DeConcini, D-Ariz.
Dave Durenberger, R-Minn.
Harlan Mathews, D-Tenn.
Howard M. Metzenbaum, D-Ohio
George Mitchell, D-Maine
Donald W. Riegle Jr., D-Mich
Malcolm Wallop, R-Wyo.

Defeated Members

House of Representatives

Peter W. Barca, D-Wis.
Tom J. Barlow, D-Ky.
James H. Bilbray, D-Nev.
Lucien Blackwell, D-Pa.
Jack Brooks, D-Texas
Leslie D. Byrne, D-Va.
Maria E. Cantwell, D-Wash.
Butler Derrick, D-S.C.
Karan English, D-Ariz.
Eric D. Fingerhut, D-Ohio
Thomas S. Foley, D-Wash.
Dan Glickman, D-Kan.
Dan Hamburg, D-Calif.
Jane Harman, D-Calif.

Peter Hoagland, D-Neb.
George Hochbrueckner, D-N.Y.
Jay R. Inslee, D-Wash.
Don Johnson, D-Ga.
Herbert C. Klein, D-N.J.
Mike Kreidler, D-Wash.
H. Martin Lancaster, D-N.C.
Larry LaRocco, D-Idaho
Richard H. Lehman, D-Calif.
David A. Levy, R-N.Y.
Jill Long, D-Ind.
David S. Mann, D-Ohio
Marjorie Margolies-Mezvinsky, D-Pa.
Frank McClosky, D-Ind.
David E. Price, D-N.C.
Dan Rostenkowski, D-Ill.
William C. Sarpalius, D-Texas
Lynn Schenk, D-Calif.
Karen Shepherd, D-Utah
Neal Smith, D-Iowa
Ted Strickland, D-Ohio
Dick Swett, D-N.H.
Mike Synar, D-Okla.
Jolene Unsoeld, D-Wash.
Craig Washington, D-Texas

Senate

Jim Sasser, D-Tenn.
Harris Wofford, D-Pa.

Members Elected
To Other Offices

House of Representatives

Rodney D. Grams, R-Minn.

James M. Inhofe, R-Okla.
Jon L. Kyl, R-Ariz.
Thomas J. Ridge, R-Pa.
Rick Santorum, R-PA
Olympia Snowe, R-Maine
Don Sundquist, R-Tenn.
Craig Thomas, R-Wyo.

Members Who Ran for
Other Offices and Lost

House of Representatives

Michael A. Andrews, D-Texas
Thomas H. Andrews, D-Maine
Helen Delich Bentley, R-Md.
Bob Carr, D-Mich.
Jim Cooper, D-Tenn.
Sam Coppersmith, D-Ariz.
Fred Grandy, R-Iowa
Michael Huffington, R-Calif.
Ron Machtley, R-R.I.
Dave McCurdy, D-Okla.
Arthur Ravenel Jr., R-S.C.
Jim Slattery, D-Kan.
Alan Wheat, D-Mo.

Members Who Died

House of Representatives

Dean A. Gallo, R-N.J.

Members Who Resigned

Senate

David L. Boren, D-Okla.

Index